FISHING THE BIG BEND

Inshore Saltwater

Volume II in the Big Bend Series

**by Bob McGowan
and
Richard Farren**

1

ISBN 0-9632059-1-9

Library of Congress Catalog Card Number: 93—60545

Published by
Woodland Productions
2208 Hickory Court
Tallahassee, FL 32311.

First Edition

Printed in the United States by
Artcraft Printers
Tallahassee, FL

Edited by Claudia Farren

2

About The Authors

Bob McGowan is a true fishermen. One of those rare individuals who catches fish where few others can, and catches more than most. There's hardly a section of coastline, or stretch of river in the Big Bend he hasn't explored and fished, over and over; always searching for the right combination of tackle and conditions for the best chance of success.

As the owner of the Tackle Box for seven years, Bob provided this hard-earned knowledge to anyone who came by with a question. As a result, he's been the subject of hundreds of fishing articles, fishing reports and television shows on fishing in the Big Bend area. Bob has been featured in *Florida Sportsman Magazine, Florida Wildlife Magazine, the Tallahassee Democrat, Woods N' Water, and Tallahassee Magazine.* He has also been a featured guest on *Big Bend Outdoors.*

Richard Farren is an outdoor writer and photographer who has been writing on the Tallahassee area for seven years. Hundreds of his articles and photographs have appeared in state, regional and national publications. He covers the outdoors as an Outdoor Correspondent for the *Tallahassee Democrat* and is an Editor-at-Large for *Florida Sportsman Magazine.* Richard is also editor of the *Florida Fish and Wildlife News,* a publication of the Florida Wildlife Federation and the *Outdoor Guides News,* a publication of the Outdoor Guides Association of North America. He is a member of the Florida Outdoor Writers Association and the Outdoor Writers Association of America.

Table of Contents

4

Table of Contents

Acknowledgements

The authors would like to thank the many friends who spent hours and hours going fishing or talking fishing. Some of them showed us their favorite methods for catching fish. Others took us to their favorite "hot spots," or simply lent us their advice about where to find the fish. In one way or another, however, every one of them has contributed to this book. They include: Eddie McGowan, Dick Husband, Allen Carter, Ben Dean, Mike Recupero, Phil Schneider, Chuck Shields, Tim Schroeder, Jim Schroeder, Jimmy Higgins, Pat McGriff, Jim Atkins, Steve Etts, Bud Reichel, Paddy Pillow, Bruce Burr, Bill Farren, Dean Losey, and Sal Guastella to name a few, and of course a special note of gratitude to Doris McGowan and Claudia Farren.

Introduction

The Big Bend area of Florida is blessed with an incredible variety of near-shore saltwater fishing opportunities. Redfish stalk the rock piles and oyster bars, seatrout roam and hunt the seagrass beds, cobia lurk in the shadows of pilings and sunken ships, and schools of Spanish mackerel scour the bait-laden waters just offshore.

Nearly two hundred miles of undeveloped, saltmarsh-dominated coastline is largely responsible for the area's fine fishing. Most of the coastline is in public ownership through a combination of state and federal agencies. With careful management of the resources, this protected habitat can provide good meals and fun times for many generations to come.

This book is designed to provide basic, useful information on the most popular inshore, saltwater species. You won't find material on amberjack or grouper fishing or trolling for king mackerel. We decided instead to concentrate on places and methods for catching saltwater gamefish found near shore; that includes redfish, seatrout, Spanish mackerel, flounder, black sea bass, mangrove snapper, bluefish, cobia and sheepshead.

If you're new to saltwater fishing in the Big Bend, we think this book will open up a whole new world of superb outings. If you're an experienced fisherman in the area, you're bound to get a few ideas to try next time you feel the urge to wet-a-line, or try a new place.

We would also like to point out that all degree headings and loran coordinates in this book are as accurate as we have been able to determine. However, a wise boat captain will always carry official navigation charts and never rely on one source of information.

The Authors

7

A Word About Tides

Following The Tides Will Improve Your Odds

It looks like you're going to have a day this weekend to go fishing. A glance at the weather report shows the high tide will be at 2 p.m. Should you get up early and be on the water at sunrise, or wait for the afternoon tide?

Although it depends on where you plan to fish, both answers are probably wrong.

The simple fact is, fish move with the tide and feed with the tide. How far, how fast, and for how long depends on a number of predictable factors, only one of which is the time of high and low tide.

For example, the tides in Apalachee Bay and other Big Bend rivers are described as "mixed" tides, meaning there are two highs and two lows every 24 hours, but the various tides rise and fall to different levels. The difference between each high and low tide is called the "range."

The greater the range between the tides, the faster the tidal current. In addition, the speed of the current varies within a tide cycle. It's strongest during the middle two hours of the cycle and slower near low and high tide.

As a general rule, the stronger the tidal flow—the better the fishing.

Put into practical terms, gamefish will usually move to feeding grounds when the tidal velocity reaches its peak during an in-coming or out-going tide. The stronger current gives the larger fish an advantage over its prey, which can be helpless when caught in the swift water.

The strongest tides, called "spring tides" (no connection to the season) occur twice a month when the moon and the sun are in line with the earth; which is during the full moon and the new moon. The weakest tides, called neap tides, occur twice a month during the first and third quarter of the moon phases, when the sun and moon are perpendicular to each other.

In addition, on a daily basis, with the "mixed" tidal system of Apalachee Bay, one set of tides within a 24-hour period can be much stronger than the other. You'll stand a better chance of success if you can consistently fish the stronger of the two. Barometric pressure, wind velocity, and wind direction can also influence the tides. According to the *Florida Sportsman Tide Atlas*, the barometric pressure can sway the tidal range by as much as six inches, which in-turn affects the tidal current. A low barometric pressure allows for a higher tide and vice-versa.

The wind can have an even more significant affect, especially when it blows steadily from one direction for long periods of time. For instance, a strong northerly wind can hold back the rising Gulf tide and increase the velocity of the falling tide. On the other hand, an onshore wind can bring the tide in much sooner than predicted and with more velocity.

Understanding the tides is especially important when fishing in the coastal rivers and creeks. In general, fish inside the creek during a rising tide, and around the mouth of the creek during a falling tide. In either case, the stronger the current, the better chance there is of finding fish.

Another point to remember is that fish react quickly to a change in tide. If redfish, for instance, are going to leave a creek during low tide, they might exit as soon as the tide turns and not wait for the water to fall. Or, they might run up a creek with the very first movement of a rising tide, even before there's enough water to follow in a boat.

In some local creeks, if there's enough water, redfish will stay inside through the low tide cycle, taking advantage of the concentrated baitfish. If you choose a weak tide you might be able to stay in there with them.

The falling tide also creates eddies around points and oyster bars that will draw feeding gamefish. The stronger the current, the more productive these "ambush points" can be for both the fish and the fisherman.

Tides can also be an important factor when fishing the upper St. Marks River, or any tidal river for that matter, for redfish and trout during the winter. The lowest stages of the strongest tides will concentrate the fish in less water which always improves the fishing.

During the spring, summer and fall, when trout and reds are on the flats, the velocity of the tidal current becomes very important. Seatrout may choose to feed at any time, but they will almost always be active when the current is strongest. The same is true of redfish, which will take advantage of the highest tides to forage in newly flooded areas, especially when there's a strong current.

Unfortunately, most readily available tidal information only includes times for high and low tides. By considering moon phases, however, and prevailing weather conditions you can at least predict when some of the stronger tides are likely to occur.

The tide tables available on the back page of *Woods 'N Water*, a local publication available in Big Bend tackle stores, includes tidal range figures that reveal when the tides will be higher or lower than usual, which is when the currents will be the strongest.

A Tide Atlas available from Wickstrom Publications, publishers of *Florida Sportsman Magazine* includes information on the tidal range, current strength, and the time of the maximum current in each tide cycle. Copies can be ordered from Wickstrom Publishers, Inc., 5901 SW 74 Street, Miami, FL 33143; (305) 661-4222.

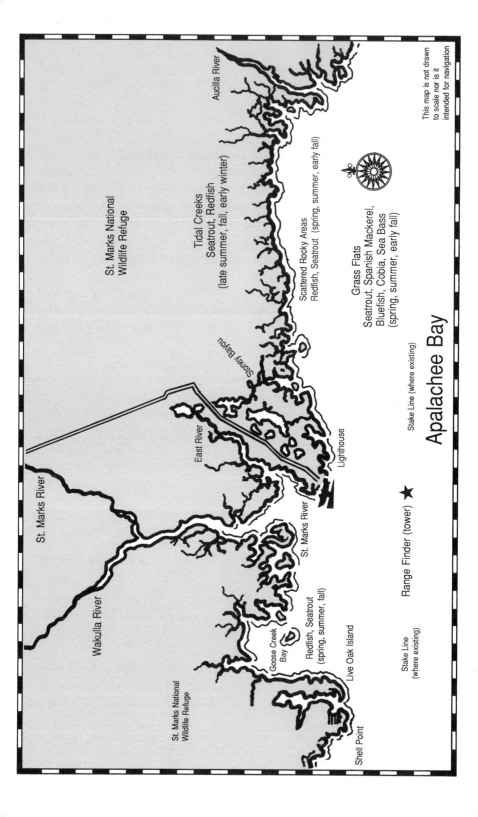

Apalachee Bay

St. Marks River

St. Marks National Wildlife Refuge

Aucilla River

Tidal Creeks
Seatrout, Redfish
(late summer, fall, early winter)

Stoney Bayou

East River

Scattered Rocky Areas
Redfish, Seatrout (spring, summer, early fall)

Grass Flats
Seatrout, Spanish Mackerel,
Bluefish, Cobia, Sea Bass
(spring, summer, early fall)

Stake Line (where existing)

St. Marks River

Lighthouse

Wakulla River

St. Marks National
Wildlife Refuge

Goose Creek
Bay

Redfish, Seatrout
(spring, summer, fall)

Live Oak Island

Shell Point

Stake Line
(where existing)

Range Finder (tower) ★

This map is not drawn
to scale nor is it
intended for navigation

Apalachee Bay

Clear water and an undisturbed habitat characterize this section of Florida's Gulf coast

Apalachee Bay is the heart of saltwater fishing in the Big Bend. Its hundreds of square miles of seagrass and salt marsh converts the sun's energy to plant matter that in turn fuels the basis for a food web that maintains a vast array of gamefish including seatrout, redfish, cobia, flounder, Spanish mackerel, king mackerel, grouper, sheepshead, bluefish, sea bass, and sharks.

The bay is a bowl-shaped depression in the coastline of the extreme northeast corner of the Gulf of Mexico. Its boundaries for the purposes of this book could more or less be described as extending from about the Steinhatchee River on the east to the Ochlockonee River on the west. It has a straight-line distance of about 50 miles, and a shoreline distance over 70 miles. A dropoff of only two feet per mile from the shoreline into the Gulf provides plenty of clear, shallow water for the development of healthy seagrass beds.

East and West Flats - seatrout

Apalachee Bay is divided by the St. Marks Ship Channel into two sections known as the East Flats and the West Flats.

A common reference point on the East Flats is the "Stake Line," which is a line of pilings that mark the outer boundary of the St. Marks Refuge. Anglers often talk about catching fish: at the "Stake Line," outside of the "Stake Line" or 1/2 mile inside of the "Stake Line."

There were a lot more "stakes" when the boundary was first established, but they've disappeared one by one over the years. Even so, the remaining stakes are useful reference points when fishing on the East Flats between the St. Marks and Aucilla rivers.

Apalachee Bay seatrout (above) and redfish (below).

Numerous small creeks are scattered along the shoreline of Apalachee Bay. In general, the creeks along the East Flats are shallow and rocky while the shoreline and creeks along the West Flats are somewhat deeper and have fewer obstructions.

Spotted seatrout are common virtually all over the grass flats of Apalachee Bay from shallow water near shore to ten-foot depths five miles offshore. They first show up in the spring when the water temperature reaches the upper sixties; and they stay until the temperature hits about the same spot on the way back down.

In general, trout fishing is better close to shore in the spring and fall, and a couple miles offshore during the heat of the summer.

Probably 95 percent of trout anglers use plastic jigs or live shrimp. And for good reason, they work. Jigs and feathers should be worked in a quick hopping motion along the bottom. Some anglers like to put a piece of shrimp on the hook to give the bait a little scent. The piece of natural bait also attracts small baitfish which in-turn will draw the attention of any nearby gamefish.

During recent years, many anglers have been turning to topwater plugs to add a little excitement to their trout fishing. Under some conditions, such as when the water is murky following a period of heavy rain, topwater can be the most effective choice. In all cases, trout are very aggressive when hitting a lure on the surface and provide great sport for the patient angler.

Live shrimp can be free-lined or fished beneath a popping cork. The biggest hinderance to either method is the hordes of pinfish that continually batter at the bait. Nevertheless, when trout fishing is slow, live shrimp can often be the most reliable option.

Small pinfish also make excellent trout bait. They can be caught with Bream Busters and tiny pieces of bait and very small hooks. Use a popping cork to keep the bait from burrowing into the grass.

[For more information on fishing the flats, see the chapters on seatrout, cobia, Spanish mackerel, and sea bass.]

Rocks Along the Coast - redfish

Large sections of the shoreline of Apalachee Bay east of the St. Marks River have a rocky, irregular bottom. There are also a number of large rock piles scattered throughout the same area, some of which extend above the surface. Most of the rock piles that are a navigation hazard to unwary boat operators begin just east of the mouth of Big Cove, which is the second small inlet along the coast east of the lighthouse. Some of the largest formations are off the mouth of Stony Bayou Creek and around the mouth of the Pinhook River.

The rocks are limestone, and very hard. They don't bend, break, move, or compromise when impacted by boat bows, outdrives, propellers or lower units. Dynamite might budge them a little, but not a boat.

Only a very few rock piles appear on navigation charts and even those locations aren't precise. Many of the piles are also marked with stakes, but not all; and there are numerous lone rocks lurking just under the surface at low tide. Most of the rocky areas or rock piles that are dangerous to navigation are within a mile and a half of the shoreline.

Following the "Stake Line" is safe for most shallow-water fishing boats at any tide. Care should be taken, however, near the mouth of the Aucilla River where the Stake Line swings closer to shore. The area is shallow and has a scattering of oyster bars. Keep one eye on the water in front of the boat and one eye on a navigation chart until you learn your way around this part of the bay.

Navigation hazards aside, the rocks are a real benefit to fishermen. Practically every rock harbors some sort of marine life. Gamefish take advantage of this fact, and so should we.

Wear polaroid glasses to cut the surface glare. They will allow you to see the bottom. Then fish around every rock or rock pile that you see. You'll be surprised at the results. Regardless of whether the structure is showing or submerged, if there's at least a foot of water, it's worth a cast or two.

Although truly the realm of the redfish, at one time or another, we've caught seatrout, rock bass, cobia, Spanish mackerel, bluefish, sharks, and flounder around the rock piles.

In some areas, particularly off Stony Bayou Creek and the Pinhook River, and also south of the Steinhatchee River, there are rocks covered with a yellow, sargasso-type seagrass known locally as "cattails." The variety of sealife, including crabs and small fish that live in the seaweed

attract plenty of predators. Sometimes you can actually see redfish with their tails out of the water and noses buried into the weeds rummaging for food the same way they do on soft bottoms.

Approach the rock piles carefully, especially on clear days. The fish spook easily in shallow water. You can even choose to anchor your boat and wade when the water is low. Wear foot protection against sharp rocks, sea urchins and sting rays.

The usual saltwater baits and lures will work—feathers, jigs, gold spoons, topwater plugs, pinfish, shiner tails, and shrimp. When the water is shallow, gold spoons or floating plugs are much easier to use. When the fish are lurking in the seaweed, a live shrimp dropped right in the middle won't survive for long. [For more information see the chapter on redfish.]

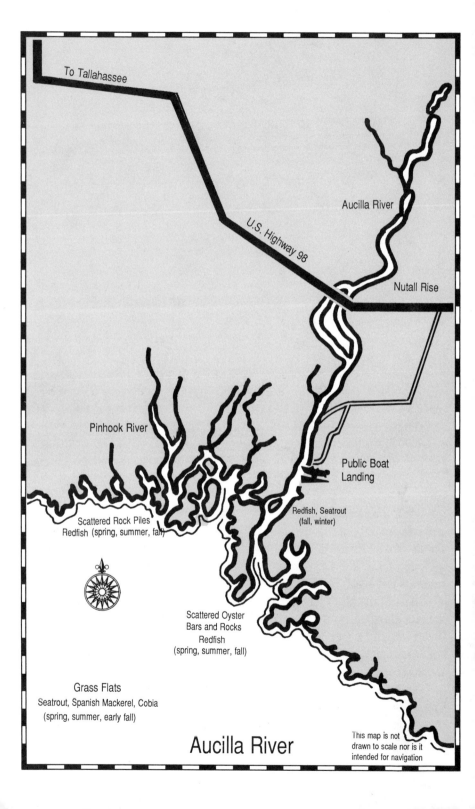

Aucilla River

Good fishing at an out of the way spot

The Aucilla River begins in southern Georgia and flows 70 miles to Apalachee Bay. About ten miles from the Gulf of Mexico the river is captured by a sinkhole. It re-emerges five miles closer to the coast near the small settlement of Nutall Rise. Only the lower five miles of the river hold any interest to saltwater fishermen.

Unfortunately, the lower river poses a serious navigation hazard to the boater. There are numerous places where oyster bars or limestone outcroppings lay just inches below the surface. Increasing the difficulty is a lack of channel markers, buoys, or stakes, to warn boaters of dangerous territory. Many anglers learn the hard way.

The navigable channel, or what there is of one, doesn't follow the shape of the river. Instead, it crosses from one side to the other at random, and with nothing to indicate when it's going to change direction.

On the Flats

While the gamefish are on the flats, the Aucilla River provides access to a part of Apalachee Bay that has less fishing pressure than the area around the St. Marks River. The grass flats are similar to other parts of the bay, although there is a large area of spotty bottom (intermittent patches of seagrass and sand) off the mouth of the river.

Some of the best fishing in the area can be found immediately west of the Aucilla off the mouth of the Pinhook River. (The Pinhook is the third outlet west of the Aucilla.) There are a number of grass-covered rocky areas near the mouth that are very attractive to redfish and trout especially during fall and early winter.

During a medium to low tide, redfish can sometimes be seen burrowing into the seagrasses looking for small fish and crustaceans.

The combination of rocks and seaweed can make lure fishing very

19

difficult. To avoid spooking the fish away from the structure, cast beyond the rocks and work the lure back through the area. As an alternative try staying well back from the rocks and lobbing a big, live shrimp or small pinfish right into the middle and let it sit. It won't be there for long.

There are also broad sandy basins in a couple spots near the Pinhook that flounder are attracted to. Work a large red or white jig tipped with a piece of shrimp slowly along the bottom, moving it only two or three feet at a time. Look for deeper areas with a sandy or even muddy bottom. Flounder will also rise off the bottom to attack a slow moving crankbait such as a sinking MirrOlure.

In the River

Every year, usually beginning in late September or early October, the Aucilla comes alive with seatrout and redfish. The fish generally stay inside the river all winter, but the first months are the best.

Although gamefish can be caught all the way up to U.S. Highway 98, the most consistently productive area is from just below the island in the lower river up to about a half mile above the lower landing. Water depths in this portion of the river vary from a few inches up to 15 feet. A depth finder can save you a lot of time and effort in trying to locate the river channel and holes between limerock channels.

When the fish are in the river concentrate your fishing around the limestone ledges, drop-offs, and bends in the river channel. There is very little vegetation to contend with, just the rocks.

Also, there is usually a hole downriver of most oyster bars and limestone outcroppings. A good approach is to drop a live shrimp or pinfish into the deeper of these holes. Use a 1/2 to 1-ounce egg sinker, depending on line size, to hold bottom against the current. Be sure to use an 18-inch steel leader or monofilament leader of at least 30 to 40 pound test.

If nothing develops in the hole you've chosen, try drifting downstream while fishing with artificials until you come upon the next likely looking hole. Then drop an anchor and try another live bait.

With this method a first-time visitor to the Aucilla can catch fish while learning the river and the hot spots at the same time. Use an oyster bar or clump of trees to mentally note any spot on the river in which you find activity. If you can't decide where to fish, try free-lining a pinfish anywhere in the river.

The best lure and bait choices include jigs, MirrOlures, crankbaits, gold spoons, and of course live shrimp or pinfish.

Boat Ramps

There are two public boat ramps on the lower portion of the Aucilla River.

* The Nutall Rise Landing is located about five miles from the Gulf near the Highway 98 bridge over the Aucilla River. Turn north on the first dirt road east of the bridge. The ramp is a few hundred yards from the highway.

* To reach the lower ramp, turn south off of U.S. Highway 98 one and a half miles east of the bridge over the Aucilla River. Follow the signs. The ramp is about two miles from the Gulf of Mexico. Rocks just out from the base of the ramp can damage a carelessly launched boat, especially at low tide.

We recommend boats that are 16-feet and under for use on the Aucilla. Use caution on the river at all times.

The public ramp on the lower Aucilla River can be difficult to use at low tide, and is better suited to smaller boats.

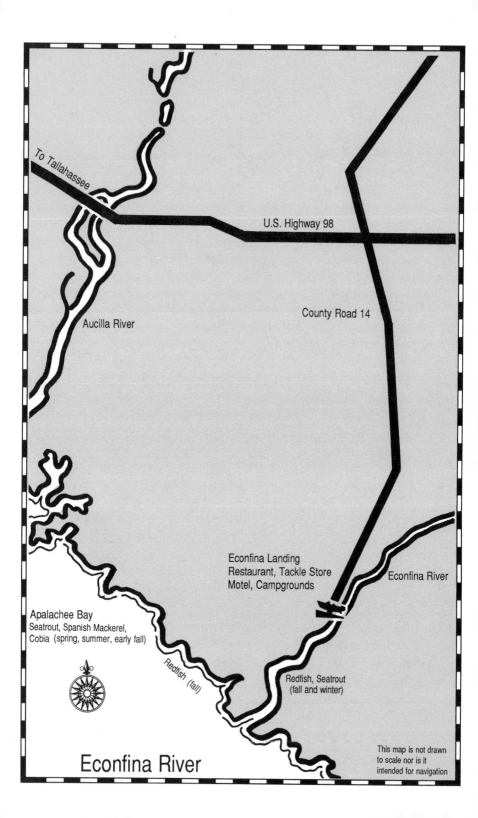

To Tallahassee

U.S. Highway 98

County Road 14

Aucilla River

Econfina Landing
Restaurant, Tackle Store
Motel, Campgrounds

Econfina River

Apalachee Bay
Seatrout, Spanish Mackerel,
Cobia (spring, summer, early fall)

Redfish (fall)

Redfish, Seatrout
(fall and winter)

This map is not drawn
to scale nor is it
intended for navigation

Econfina River

Econfina River

Go Down East For Some Good Fishing

About 60 miles southeast of Tallahassee, the Econfina represents a little piece of untainted Florida — a pristine, black water, "southern" river, that emerges from a swampy area in Madison County known as San Pedro Bay and flows about 35 miles to the Gulf.

Habitat is what makes good fishing, and the Econfina River enters the Gulf right in the middle of the longest stretch of public-owned coastal habitat in Florida. Eventually over 200 miles of this largely undisturbed coastal marsh and coastal forest will be forever protected. A 4,000 acre parcel of undeveloped forest around the lower river has also been acquired by the state and is being turned into a state park.

There are a few houses, a motel and a fish camp on the river near a public boat ramp that gives access to the eastern end of Apalachee Bay.

The ramp is about two miles from the mouth of the river, but it's not as simple as jumping in the boat and running down the river. The dark water hides limestone rock ledges and outcroppings that can bring an early end to your fishing trip, especially during a low tide.

Ask the folks in the tackle store for directions on getting safely down the river. And as a precaution, go slow, and sign out in the log book with your time of departure and expected return.

Except for a few cabins along the lower river, the Econfina is bordered by a thick hardwood forest. Live oaks stretch their moss-covered branches over the water, and tall, skinny sable palms tower over the shoreline vegetation. Mature pines and palmetto bushes dot the river banks.

About a mile from the Gulf the trees give way to a wide expanse of saltmarsh. Look for an eagle's nest a few hundred yards to the south in a tree standing in the marsh. A bald eagle can often be seen sitting on a nearby branch.

Oyster bars across the mouth of the river increase the navigation problem, but a series of PVC stakes mark a shallow channel. Follow the stakes carefully, and slowly, especially at low tide.

The eastern end of Apalachee Bay is similar to the area off the St. Marks River. A shallow, gently sloping, seagrass-covered bottom extends away from shore. From just off the mouth of the river you can spot Rock Island about seven miles to the southeast. The island is about a mile offshore and makes a good reference point if you're fishing in that direction.

If it's your first time in this part of the bay it might be a good idea to drift the flats at least a mile or two offshore while watching to see how the "regulars" get around. From March through November the flats hold the usual variety of gamefish: seatrout, Spanish mackerel, cobia, and redfish.

Seatrout

Like most of Apalachee Bay, spotted seatrout roam the seagrass beds for one to three miles offshore from approximately March through November. Shrimp or plastic jigs are the standard bait choices for seatrout and about anything else that's around.

During winter when a large number of trout enter the shallow river many anglers switch to hot-pink, floating or slow-sinking MirrOlures. The topwater lure should be worked with a "walking the dog motion" like you would a Zara Spook. You can expect more action with a fast moving lure. When using a slow-sinking lure, from the 52M series, allow it to sink several feet before retrieving if depths allow. It should be worked with intermittent jerks or twitches to resemble an injured minnow.

Spanish mackerel

This part of Apalachee Bay seems to always draw an abundance of Spanish mackerel, but there is no channel to attract them like off the St. Marks River. If you see bird activity or surface activity it's likely to be mackerel tearing into a school of bait. All you have to do is get there before the action stops and get a lure into the water. A calmer approach would be to troll silver spoons in the vicinity until the mackerel find you!

Cobia

Cobia, for the most part are caught by accident while fishing for seatrout on the flats. There isn't much in the way of structure near the Econfina that concentrate the free-roaming fish. If your wind and tide-driven drift is slow enough you can put a small pinfish out behind the boat. Chances are good a cobia or shark will find it.

Redfish

Redfish in the Econfina area tend to stay close to shore where they feed around oyster bars and rocky areas. As the tide rises you can work your way carefully towards shore, how close depends on how big your boat is. If you're comfortable moving close to shore, look for reds aroung the many creek mouths in the area. Gold spoons, jigs, and pinfish can be effective.

Boat Ramp and Facilities

The Econfina River boat ramp is at the end of State Highway 14 which crosses Highway 98 about four miles east of the bridge over the Aucilla River. The double ramp is in excellent condition and has docks on both sides. There's a camp store/tackle store and a restaurant nearby.

If you care to make a weekend of it, *Econfina on the Gulf* has motel rooms and efficiency apartments. R/V and tent camping sites are also available and there's a conference center for mixing business and pleasure. For information and reservations contact *Econfina On The Gulf*, Rt. 1, Box 255, Lamont, FL 32336; tel. 904-584-5811.

Boat ramp on the Econfina River.

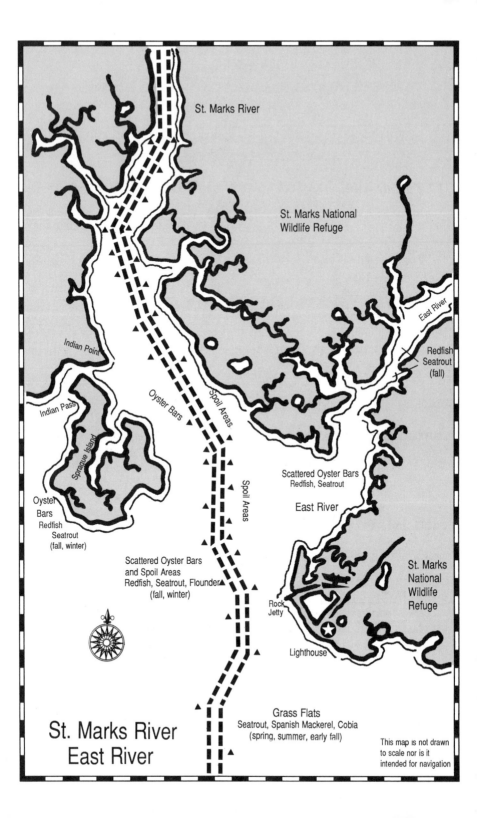

St. Marks River

St. Marks National
Wildlife Refuge

East River

Redfish
Seatrout
(fall)

Indian Point

Oyster Bars

Spoil Areas

Indian Pass

Sprague Island

Spoil Areas

Scattered Oyster Bars
Redfish, Seatrout

East River

Oyster
Bars
Redfish
Seatrout
(fall, winter)

Scattered Oyster Bars
and Spoil Areas
Redfish, Seatrout, Flounder
(fall, winter)

St. Marks
National
Wildlife
Refuge

Rock
Jetty

Lighthouse

Grass Flats
Seatrout, Spanish Mackerel, Cobia
(spring, summer, early fall)

St. Marks River
East River

This map is not drawn
to scale nor is it
intended for navigation

East River

This lightly visited river holds good fishing for the adventurous angler

The East River exists largely within the St. Marks National Wildlife Refuge. It was dammed in the 1930s creating the East River Pool, a reservoir of freshwater used to adjust the salinity of other pools in the refuge.

During periods of heavy rain, excess water flows over a spillway in the reservoir and into the lower river. From there the small river meanders in a southwesterly direction through the saltmarsh, gradually widening until it joins the St. Marks River near Channel Marker Number 14.

The East River has an abundance of oyster bars, sand bars, and mud flats with a narrow, natural channel that winds between them. There are no channel markers or buoys for guidance. The best time to learn how to navigate the river is at low tide when the oyster bars are exposed. Even then you should use a chart and be wary of shallow water and abandoned crab traps.

There are scattered oyster bars from the mouth of the river to Pelican Point, which is where the river narrows into a typical tidal stream with a number of smaller branches meandering off into the marsh. This narrow section of the river is very shallow, especially during low tide.

If winds and tides are favorable, one way to fish the river is to drift with the current while using feathers, jigs, gold spoons, or shrimp. Work the edge of oyster bars and cast around the openings to the smaller creeks where fish tend to feed.

At times the deeper holes between the oyster bars can be very productive. If you find fish in a hole, anchor nearby as quietly as possible and continue to fish the same spot. There is a limited amount of deep water in the East River and fish can be heavily concentrated at times.

Seatrout

Seatrout can be caught in the East River year-round, but the best time is in the fall when the water temperature first begins to drop. The most productive months are usually from mid-September to December.

When the water temperature drops into the mid-60's most of the trout will abandon the East River in favor of the larger and slightly warmer St. Marks and Wakulla Rivers. During warm winters, trout will stay in the East River until spring.

Look for seatrout anywhere in the river with at least three to four feet of water. Excellent catches have come from as far upriver as Pelican Point during the cooler months.

Fish the strongest currents of each tide, and if possible the strongest tide cycle. For seatrout, concentrate more towards the center of the river channel where the current is strongest.

Use MirrOlures, jigs, and live shrimp. Topwater lures like 21M series MirrOlures or a Bomber Rip Shad can be affective on trout before the water temperature gets too low. Pink, chartreuse, or red and white are popular color choices for any of the lures.

If the current is strong, try free-lining a shrimp with a single split-shot. Allow the bait to move with the current as unimpeded by the line as possible. During slack tide, use a popping cork to hold the bait off the bottom.

Redfish

Redfish can be caught in the East River anytime of the year especially around the oyster bars near the confluence with the St. Marks River. Like seatrout, however, reds will move up-river when the water temperature begins to drop in the fall.

Concentrate on oyster bars and along the shoreline. Also watch for redfish on the mud flats during low tide. Above the oyster bars where the East River narrows, look for reds around the mouths of tributary creeks, especially during a falling tide.

Redfish will hit live shrimp or pinfish as well as jigs and topwater plugs. One of the most reliable lures, as always, is a 1/4 or 1/2-ounce weedless Johnson gold spoon.

Among the advantages of using spoons is casting accuracy and distance. They also allow you to cover a lot of water while drifting with the current. Rigged with a ball bearing swivel a spoon should be retrieved just fast enough to make the blade flutter. Place a swivel only 12 to 18 inches above the lure and use 20 to 25-pound monofilament leader because of the oyster bars and the sandpaper mouth of a redfish.

Anglers in the East River often anchor next to the marsh grass and fish for trout in the deeper water in the center of the stream.

Bottom Fish

Sheepshead and black drum can be caught on occasion in the deeper holes of the East River, especially during the cooler months. Cut bait, frozen shrimp, fiddler crabs, and fresh shrimp will all catch fish, but you can expect to spend a lot of time gingerly removing pinfish from your hook. Use about a 1/0 or 2/0 hook, and an egg sinker heavy enough to keep it on the bottom in the current.

Other Species

Ladyfish, sand seatrout, jack crevalle, bluefish, and Spanish mackerel are also occasional visitors to the East River.

Sand seatrout will venture upriver about as far as speckled trout, and will hit the same types of lures. If you happen upon a school of sand trout switch to a smaller jig or even a small spoon or freshwater spinner.

Spanish mackerel, ladyfish, and bluefish can occasionally be caught during the spring and summer near the mouth of the East River where it intersects the St. Marks River. The area is always worth a few casts, especially on days when the flats are "white-capping."

29

Keaton Beach guide, Pat McGriff, specializes in live bait fishing and has a knack for finding seatrout.

Small pinfish are a very effective seatrout bait.

Keaton Beach

Seatrout, redfish, and scallops

About 20 miles southwest of Perry, on the eastern edge of Apalachee Bay, Keaton Beach is a little piece of old Florida—a small rustic-looking fishing village on an overlooked part of the Gulf Coast. It's complete with a marina that has motel rooms and cottages for rent, a boat hoist and a boat ramp. A second marina was destroyed in the March 1993, "storm of the century."

There is a small "beach" at Keaton Beach, but the real attraction is the endless miles of saltmarsh and seagrass. This largely undisturbed habitat is the basis for the excellent redfish and seatrout fishing that greets the visiting angler.

Fishing approaches for all species are similar to what's found in the chapters on Steinhatchee and Apalachee Bay. You can drift the flats offshore or work in close towards the creeks and small bays.

There is one method of flats fishing that as far as we know originated in Keaton Beach and is worthy of mention, both for use there and anywhere else there's a wide expanse of seagrass in shallow water.

Seatrout and Redfish—McGriff Style

Keaton Beach fishing guide, Pat McGriff, has a unique system for catching seatrout and redfish in the grass beds off Keaton Beach. He employs fishing skill, live bait and a little specialized knowledge. If you've ever spent time drifting and fishing the flats with live bait, you soon learn that the best way to fish is to cast off either end of the boat and slightly ahead of the drift. That gives the bait time to sit undisturbed by the movement of the boat. You may also have noticed that fish often strike somewhere near the point where the bait begins to swing in line behind the drifting boat.

One possible explanation is that the gamefish sense the bait and move in for a closer look. When the bait suddenly picks up speed from the pull of the boat a watching gamefish can't help but go for it.

McGriff refers to this area as the "sweet spot" and his approach is to place as many baits as possible for as long as possible in that spot.

He has seven rod holders mounted along one rail of his 19-0 foot boat. While drifting across the shallow flats, his clients begin by casting a live bait, rigged with a popping cork and splitshot, off each end of the boat. After popping the cork a couple times the rods are dropped into the inside rod holders.

The process continues as two more baits are cast off either end of the boat and the rods placed in the next holder over. The baits follow each other through the sweet spot then fall in-line behind the boat. Eventually the inside rods are retrieved and the baits returned to the starting point. The other rods are shifted over creating an empty rod holder at the end. Essentially, McGriff's clients are parading a steady stream of baitfish through the "sweet spot," off each end of the boat.

When the procedure is working, you're effectively covering at least a 150-foot swath with multiple baits. When the gamefish start finding the baits, it draws the attention of other fish, and the activity builds upon itself. This can lead to some of the fastest action you'll ever encounter on the flats.

If you stay close to shore, in less than three feet of water, you can even catch a mix of trout and redfish.

Either shrimp or pinfish will work, but with shrimp you might have to cut back on the number of rods because of attacking baitfish. Pinfish, on the other hand, stay on the hook until removed by you or a gamefish.

You can catch pinfish right out of the same grass that you're fishing in. Use a very small gold hook, at least a number 6 or 8, and bait it with a tiny piece of mullet or chicken gizzard or a piece of Probait.

Pinfish used to catch seatrout and redfish should be fairly small, somewhere between an inch and an inch and a half long. McGriff prefers using pinfish about the same width as a silver dollar. To catch a pinfish that size you have to place a matchhead-sized piece of bait just over the barb, anything larger will attract pinfish too large to use for bait.

Drop the tiny piece of bait directly into the grass, then pull it slowly back up. If there's any pinfish around, they'll find it immediately.

Location

To get to Keaton Beach, turn southwest off U.S. Highway 98 onto State Highway 361, a couple miles south of Perry. The road runs directly into Keaton Beach. The marina is on a canal that exits to a navigation channel leading offshore. Pat McGriff can be reached at (904) 578-2699. See page 112 for more information.

32

The shallow waters near Keaton Beach generally supply a bountiful population of scallops. Inquire at the local marina on the availability of the current crop and on good places to look. A saltwater fishing license is required when harvesting scallops with the use of a boat. Snorklers are also required to fly a "Divers Down" flag when anyone is in the water. The daily limit per person is five gallons of uncleaned scallops or 1/2 gallon of cleaned meat.

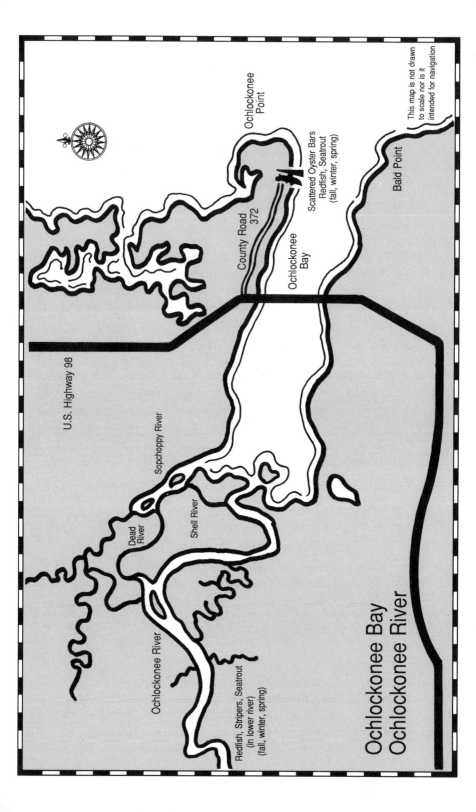

Ochlockonee Point

Ochlockonee Bay

County Road 372

Scattered Oyster Bars
Redfish, Seatrout
(fall, winter, spring)

Bald Point

This map is not drawn to scale nor is it intended for navigation

U.S. Highway 98

Sopchoppy River

Dead River

Shell River

Ochlockonee River

Redfish, Stripers, Seatrout
(in lower river)
(fall, winter, spring)

Ochlockonee Bay
Ochlockonee River

Ochlockonee River

Including Ochlockonee Bay

As in most of the rivers along the Big Bend coast, large numbers of saltwater gamefish move into the Ochlockonee every fall and winter in search of milder water temperatures. The regulars include spotted seatrout, sand seatrout, redfish, flounder, sheepshead, black drum, mangrove snapper, and striped bass.

The Ochlockonee River widens into Ochlockonee Bay a few miles from the Gulf of Mexico. Oyster bars are scattered throughout the bay and navigation requires some careful attention. The main river channel through the bay more or less splits into two outlets as it nears the Gulf. The south channel swings to the south near Bald Point and continues on past Lighthouse Point. On the other side of the bay, the channel moves northerly toward Ochlockonee Point and then flows in an easterly direction into Apalachee Bay.

Above the Highway 98 bridge the natural channel again splits. The channel on the north side is marked all the way up to Bayside Marina, and continues on (unmarked) into the Sopchoppy River. The channel to the south, which is not marked, continues in a westerly direction into the Ochlockonee River.

Redfish

Redfish are creatures of habit. They like to feed in the same spots at the same tide and will keep that appointment day after day, season after season. Once you've identified a number of these "meeting places," you'll have a pattern to follow that will greatly increase your chances of success. Unfortunately, since these "hot spots" are usually closely guarded by those that know them, most of us have to go out and find our own and Ochlockonee Bay is a good place to start looking. The obvious approach is to move around stopping for a few minutes at every likely looking spot. Every time you catch a redfish take note of the tide.

Since implementation of strict redfish conservation measures, many anglers have discovered the fun of catch and release.

Redfish prefer to feed around some type of structure—rocks, points of land, oyster bars, creek mouths, pilings, and even shorelines draw their attention.

At high tide, redfish will roam across the bars, snuffling for food along the bottom. At low tide, look for them where the tidal flow is squeezed between two emerging bars, or where the current sweeps around the end of a bar.

Try working a chartreuse-colored jig over the submerged oyster bars. Don't drag the lure, it will only hang up on the oysters. Hold the rod tip high and hop the lure a few inches at a time. You might want to add a piece of shrimp to the hook to give it a little odor.

A couple of oyster bars can be fished from the beach at Bald Point. Try casting jigs, or live shrimp with a heavily weighted popping cork upcurrent of the bars and let it drift through the feeding zone.

To reach Bald Point turn southeast off of U.S. Highway 98 onto the first paved road south of the river. Turn left at the next paved road to the left and drive to the end of the road.

Look to the Creeks

Further inland from the mouth of the bay are a number of creeks that attract redfish in the winter. In general, reds move into the creeks with the rising tide and out with the falling tide. Because creeks vary in size and depth, redfish may choose different times to enter and leave different creeks. A good way to start is by floating a live shrimp or pinfish around the mouth of any of the creeks.

About one mile west of Bald Point, on the south side of the bay, Big Chaires Creek turns to the south and splits up into smaller creeks. This once well-guarded secret spot isn't so secret anymore, but it still contains some of the best seatrout and redfish fishing in the Big Bend country during the fall and early winter.

Both the upper Ochlockonee and the Sopchoppy rivers attract saltwater species in the fall and winter, but the deeper and wider Ochlockonee usually holds the better fishing.

Saltwater gamefish will sometimes travel upriver as far as 25 miles from the Gulf. Ochlockonee River State Park is a little over 14 miles inland and is a good place to launch a boat for winter fishing. Womack Creek is about as far upriver as you would ever want to look for saltwater species.

Redfish normally will venture farther upriver than any of the other saltwater species. As noted earlier, look for reds at the mouth of any of the tributary creeks, but pay special attention to Cow Creek, Yankee John Creek, Bear Creek, Crooked River and the Dead River. Also fish the bends in the river, especially those where the current has scoured deep holes.

There are several places in the lower Ochlockonee that are over 25 feet deep. Look for redfish and stripers in these holes in the winter.

Fishing Methods

Trolling in the lower Ochlockonee River can be very rewarding at times and is an excellent way to cover a lot of water while locating fish. Deep diving crankbaits like Bagley's DB3, the Dredge, and Mann's 20+ are good lure choices.

Best colors to use are Tennessee shad, or crawfish, since the river is full of both of these prey species. Other colors can also work well at times — baby bass, perch, and silver are good choices. It's also a good idea to take along a lure retriever of some type. You don't have to lose very many $5 lures to realize the value of a retriever.

Use shallow running crankbaits in depths of 10 - 15 feet or less and troll as slow as possible to get the lure down to its maximum depth.

Try to position the boat to move with the tide. Fish can be caught while trolling against the tide, but the lure will be less effective. Gamefish tend to hunt against the tidal flow allowing food to be swept their way.

When you catch a fish, throw a marker buoy over the side, or find a reference point on the shore. Troll back over the spot two or three times or drift fish with a jigging spoon or plastic jig. Be sure the lure reaches the bottom between hops. Countdown lures are also good to use when casting to a selected spot. Rat-L-Traps, Cordell Spots, Sugar Shad, and Rapala make effective countdown lures.

Another approach is to use a live shrimp rigged with a 1/2-ounce or larger slip-sinker depending on the current. Use a monofilament leader and place the sinker above the swivel. Run the line through a slip cork and slip a small splitshot on the line above the bobber so that the sinker stops a foot or two above the bottom. The shrimp will then drift out behind the sinker, wavering in the current a few inches from the bottom.

Striped Bass

The Ochlockonee River is second only to the Apalachicola River in having the largest population of striped bass found in any of the Big Bend rivers.

Although it once contained a native population, the stripers are in the Ochlockonee largely as a result of over a decade of stocking programs in Lake Talquin. Occasional flooding washes the fish through the Jackson Bluff Dam and into the lower river. By the end of the 1980's, biologists had found evidence that the stripers were again successfully reproducing in the lower Ochlockonee.

In the spring, if there's been enough rain, striped bass make a 67-mile spawning run upriver all the way to the dam. During much of the rest of the year, and especially in the winter, they can be caught in the deepest holes near the mouth of the river. Another good striper spot we've found is around the pilings of the abandoned railroad trestle crossing the Ochlockonee just below the mouth of the Crooked River.

For striper fishing use white, four to six-inch grubs or curly-tailed plastic worms with a 1/2-ounce to 3/4-ounce lead-headed jig. They'll also hit large, white bucktail feathers rigged with a worm trailer.

Trolling with shallow to medium running crankbaits can sometimes work in deeper sections of the river. When casting crankbaits, be sure they bump into the bottom during the retrieve.

Fishing with live bait, however, is the most consistent approach to catching striped bass in about any situation. With little hesitation, striped bass will pounce upon any helpless meal that happens their way including wild and commercial shiners, shad and small bream. **(Florida state fishing regulations require that a bream used for bait must have been caught on a hook and line.)**

In the winter, place a live bait in any of the deep holes in the lower river. Use the method described above for fishing with live shrimp in the river. In the early spring use live baits with a popping cork around the area where the river meets the bay.

Striped bass are very aggressive hunters, especially in the spring when they work hard to put on weight lost during slow feeding times in the winter.

The Ochlockonee Shoals are a great location for hunting cobia.

Ochlockonee Shoals

This shallow, offshore area attracts hordes of gamefish

The Ochlockonee Shoals is a large, kidney-shaped sand and grass reef located about six miles southwest of the Number 1 Sea Buoy marking the end of the ship channel out of the St. Marks River. The shallows are about four miles long and two miles wide at the widest point. The shallowest spot, which is near the center of the shoals is about three feet deep during low tide.

A mixture of seagrasses including turtle grass, eelgrass, and manatee grass grow in abundance around the perimeter of the reef. The vegetation grows more sparsely in the shallower areas creating a patchy bottom of seagrass and sand. Large fish such as sharks and cobia can often be sighted against the light-colored background.

In addition to fishing, the shoals are also a good spot for shallow water activities like swimming, snorkeling, and scuba diving for the beginner.

Fishing the Shoals

Spanish mackerel, bluefish, blue runners, jack crevalle, ladyfish, cobia, king mackerel, and sharks cruise the waters around and over the shoals. Most of the gamefish begin appearing in the late spring when the surf temperature rises into the 70s. Spanish and king mackerel usually show up first along with hordes of ladyfish (skipjacks). Within a couple of weeks the rest of the gamefish contingent comes on the scene.

The fishing stays good throughout the summer until about late October. The best times to fish the shoals has more to do with water clarity than water temperature. If visibility is poor, it's difficult to troll or cast in relation to the bottom structure. On bad days, usually following long periods of rainy or windy weather, the depth finder can be reading three feet but you can't see the bottom over the side of the boat. Even on good days, a pair of polarized sunglasses are essential for spotting fish through the surface glare.

One of the most popular fishing approaches used at the Ochlockonee Shoals is trolling with spoons, plain jigs, or jigs with added strips of natural-bait cut from mullet, cigar minnows, or ladyfish. Troll just off the edge of the shoals until you catch something. Put out a marker buoy and circle back through the area until the fish stop hitting.

Another method is to drift while casting jigs, spoons, or MirrOlures; much like you would when fishing the flats. Pay special attention to areas that drop off into deeper water. Work your lure across different sections of the slope. In the shallower water, pull the lures along the edges of the open areas, and across the center of the grassy areas.

One of the most exciting things to do is drift a live pinfish away from the boat. Kingfish as large as 40 pounds have been caught this way at the shoals. And if the kings aren't around, there's always plenty of sharks to harass your bait; and maybe a cobia if you're lucky.

Use strong tackle and wire leader, or at least 100-pound test monofilament, when drifting a live bait. And use a 6/0 to 9/0 bait hook depending upon the size of the baitfish.

Getting There

The shoals are located about six miles from the Number One Sea Buoy out of St. Marks at a heading of 185 degrees. Loran C Coordinates for the approximate center of the shoals are 14450/46400.

U.S. Coast Guard Intracoastal Marker Number 24 sits about one mile southeast of the southern tip of the shoals. It marks the edge of safe passage for deep draft vessels.

The shoals are accessible from ramps and marinas in St. Marks, Panacea, Spring Creek, Alligator Point, Shell Point and the Ochlockonee River. See pages 112-113 for more information on boat ramps.

Spring Creek

Redfish, seatrout and spring fed waters

The small town of Spring Creek is at the end of County Road 365 which turns south off U.S. Highway 98 about five miles west of the Wakulla River. Take the right-hand fork about one and a half miles south of U.S. Highway 98.

The creek itself is about five miles long. Beginning just southwest of State Highway 375 it meanders in a southeast direction until reaching the Gulf of Mexico just west of Shell Point. The area at the mouth of the creek is known as Oyster Bay.

There are two large, freshwater springs near where the creek flows past the town of Spring Creek. During the fall and winter months the springs harbor seatrout, redfish, sand seatrout, sheepshead, black drum, flounder and gray snapper.

All the conventional lures and bait will catch fish in the winter — jigs, MirrOlures, cutbait, live shrimp, minnows, pinfish, crabs, fiddler crabs, and small mullet.

The creek channel winds between numerous oyster bars. The best time to learn the way is at low tide when you can see the bars. The channel is poorly marked with PVC and metal pipe. Pick your way carefully along the creek, especially through sections that aren't well-marked. It isn't called Oyster Bay for nothing.

But as in most things you have to take the bad with the good. And in this case, around every treacherous oyster bar there's usually a deep hole or "run-out" channel. And this my piscatorial friend is where the fish are. (Follow the same approaches to fishing oyster bars described in the chapter on the St. Marks River.)

Ramps available in the Spring Creek area are Bud's Marina and Fish Camp, in Spring Creek, and the Shell Point Marina, at Shell Point.

Steinhatchee guide, Jim Atkins, fishes the shallow waters and tidal creeks along the coast.

Steinhatchee

Redfish, sand seatrout — and a few others

If catching redfish is your passion, and it certainly is for many Big Bend anglers, you might want to consider a visit to Steinhatchee. The coastal environment of wide-open expanses of saltmarsh and seagrass beds provides excellent fishing in the waters near this small coastal community. But it's the rocky areas near shore and the large number of small tidal creeks that make it a first-class redfish haven.

Redfish

The approach to Steinhatchee redfish is fairly simple. Run out the channel until you find deep enough water to turn either north or south along the coast. Pick a spot within a mile or two of the river and turn back towards the shoreline.

Redfish prefer the shallow water close to shore. They also seem to like it if there is a tidal creek nearby. Because of the hard bottom, be cautious when you move into shallow water. Start fishing about the time you hit three feet of water, and work your way carefully towards shore from there.

Tides are an important consideration for both boat access and fish activity. Redfish are always more active when the water is moving than when it's slack. During the rising tide you can fish all the way to the marsh grass. As the tide continues to rise fish a few dozen yards into each tidal creek you pass looking for fish that have entered in search of food.

Redfish are boat shy, especially on calm days in shallow water. Try to choose a drift that takes you to your target area without using the engine. The same applies to fishing inside the creeks. If possible, drift in on the tidal current.

Redfish will hit anything from jigs to live shrimp and pinfish. In the Steinhatchee area the lure of choice by most anglers and guides is a gold spoon. Use a weedless spoon because of the grass patches in the shallow water and loose grass floating on top. For a leader use plastic-coated steel or heavy monofilament to prevent "break-offs" against the sharp limestone rocks.

For added excitement try a topwater plug like a floating MirrOlure. Work it slowly, retrieving it in short, noisy bursts. The lure should follow a zigzag path across the surface. Hits might not come as often when using topwater lures but they are far more exciting, especially in the shallow water.

There is no guarantee where the redfish might be feeding from tide to tide. They often go up the creeks in search of food, but if they don't find any, they're just as likely to turn right around and come back to the creek mouth where they can wait for something to show up in the current.

The redfish are around all year, but the fishing is at its best in the fall, particularly October and November. During winter, activity moves into the deeper holes of the Steinhatchee River. Use live baits fished on the bottom or plastic jigs fished slowly.

Redfish move into tidal creeks with the tide — but when, and how long they stay varies with every tide and every creek.

SEATROUT

Spotted Seatrout

The grass flats off Steinhatchee hold seatrout in numbers similar to other parts of Apalachee Bay. In general, drift the flats during spring, summer, and fall using the same techniques described in the Apalachee Bay and Keaton Beach chapters for spotted (speckled) seatrout. The grass flats with the best seatrout fishing begin a few hundred yards offshore and continue out for at least five miles growing gradually deeper.

During the winter, seatrout move into the river in large numbers and can be caught from a number of well-known holes. Look for all the other boats and fish nearby.

Sand Seatrout

Sand seatrout, (Cynoscion arenarius) also known as silver, white, gray, and sugar trout, are plentiful around Steinhatchee and can often be relied upon to salvage a slow day of speckled seatrout or redfish fishing.

Off Steinhatchee, sand seatrout first show up on the grass flats in the spring and stay through the fall. They inhabit deeper waters than speckled trout and will usually take up residence in the deepest areas of the grass flats. The same is generally true from Steinhatchee north and west along

Although small, sand seatrout can salvage a slow day of fishing on the flats along some areas of the Big Bend.

the coast of Apalachee Bay where they are rarely caught in less than eight feet of water.

Sand trout are usually most active in the fall when the water temperature first begins to drop. It's at this time of year they sometimes gather in large schools.

During the winter they'll venture into the deeper rivers along the coast like the Steinhatchee and St. Marks. In spring they go offshore to spawn, then move back into coastal waters.

Some of the best sand seatrout fishing out of Steinhatchee takes place in the "patchy-bottom" area around four to five miles offshore in eight to ten feet of water. One popular area is near Intracoastal Marker #18.

You might have to hunt around some to find fish; and don't waste time anywhere that the fish don't start biting right away. When you do catch a "sandie" you can drop a marker buoy and most likely catch fish in the same area all day. In some cases, a marker buoy will stay hot for days or even weeks if the weather remains consistent and the food supply holds up. Sand trout feed heavily on shrimp, small crabs, and pinfish.

Catching sand trout isn't what you would call challenging, but it is steady. When the fish are there, you can catch one on every cast and you can use all those old jigs that have been lying in the bottom of the tackle box for years. If you don't have any old jigs, use pieces of plastic worm and a small jig head of 1/8 or 1/4-ounce.

To increase your fun use light line and ultra-light tackle. Sand seatrout rarely grow to over a pound or more than 12 inches in length, but if they were pitted against their speckled cousins they would win all the light-weight bouts. They are so aggressive that very little effort is required to set the hook.

Directions

To get to Steinhatchee from the north, turn west off U.S. Highway 98 onto State Highway 361, a couple miles south of Perry. Turn left at Keaton Beach and continue south. The Steinhatchee River appears on your right as you enter the town. From the south, turn west (off of U.S. Highway 98) on State Highway 51, 17 miles north of Shamrock. The roads ends in Steinhatchee.

*Jim Atkins with a pair of sand seatrout from
the deep-water grass flats off Steinhatchee.*

There are two public ramps in Steinhatchee, the main one is on the Dixie
County side of the river in the town of Jena. Plus, the marinas on the river
have either a forklift or hoists for lowering your boat into the water.

Be sure to use a chart if you're exploring the waters around Steinhatchee
for the first time. Or you can hire a guide for the first trip or two, there are
a number of qualified fishing guides in the small town. Inquire at one of the
marinas. For more information see pages 112-113.

The St. Marks National Wildlife Refuge encompasses 32,000 acres of Apalachee Bay. Above, the refuge's most famous landmark, the St. Marks Lighthouse as seen from the bay.

St. Marks National Wildlife Refuge

Established in 1931, the St. Marks National Wildlife Refuge encompasses 65,000 acres of land and an additional 32,000 acres of Apalachee Bay. It's one of the oldest refuges in the United States.

The outer boundary in Apalachee Bay is marked by a series of pilings known locally as the "Stake Line." The pilings begin at a point just east of Gamble Point near the mouth of the Aucilla River and extend in a westerly direction about 18 miles to a point about one mile north of Live Oak Point.

The widest distance from the shore to the stake line is about 2 1/2 to 3 miles. When the "stakes" were first put in place they used to be spaced about one-half mile apart, but some have rotted away leaving the rest scattered at irregular intervals along the boundary.

Note: See separate chapters on Apalachee Bay, Tidal Creeks and the St. Marks River for information on fishing those specific areas within the refuge.

WADING AND SHORE FISHING

The refuge holds some of the few places along the Big Bend coast where anglers can catch gamefish without a boat. The most popular spots are near the lighthouse which is located at the end of County Road 59. There's a boat ramp nearby that provides access to the St. Marks River along a small canal. A rock jetty borders the boat canal and extends a couple hundred yards into the bay. At the very end of the jetty the water drops off to between 12 and 15 feet.

The jetty is fully exposed at low tide and easily accessible. It's covered at high tide and the rocks can be very slippery when wet. Water levels rise anywhere from two to four feet between low tide and high tide.

A rock jetty near the lighthouse in the St. Marks National Wildlife Refuge is one of the most popular shore-based fishing spots in the Big Bend.

During the warmer months, redfish, seatrout, gafftopsail catfish, sharks, jack crevalle, cobia and Spanish mackerel have been caught from the jetty. The deeper areas hold sheepshead and mangrove snapper.

Shrimp and plastic jigs will catch most of the gamefish species. If there's evidence of Spanish mackerel or ladyfish in the area, switch to a silver spoon. Live pinfish will have a better chance of attracting sharks or cobia.

Cut bait, pieces of fresh shrimp, and fiddler crabs will work on bottom species like mangrove snapper and sheepshead. Use just enough weight to hold the bottom and still feel the gentle bite of these sneaky fish.

When the tide is running, use a popping cork and small sinker to drift a live pinfish or shrimp away from the jetty and closer to near-by oyster bars.

Crabbing can be productive and fun from the jetty. Tie a chicken neck, or dead fish to a string and throw it 15 or 20 feet off the rocks. When you feel a slight tug, slowly pull the crab within reach of a crabnet.

Don't bother to fish in the boat canal, its shallow, has a mud bottom and normally only holds a mis-directed mullet or two. Sometimes small baitfish can be castnetted from the small basin next to the ramp.

Long Bar

About 300 yards to the east of the rock jetty is a combination oyster bar and sandbar that extends into the bay approximately 700 yards almost to Channel Marker Number 10 at the edge of the St. Marks Ship Channel. Long Bar is exposed at low tide and can be covered by as much as three or four feet of water during high tide.

On occasion, a few brave souls will walk or wade out on the bar for a better shot at fishing the shallow grass flats. Except for sheepshead and mangrove snapper, all the gamefish that can be caught from the jetty can be caught from the bar.

Some fishermen simply wade straight offshore from the lighthouse parking lot to about waist deep water. From there they you walk and fish towards the east all the way to the mouth of Sand Cove where the water is too deep to cross.

The bay's waters are also accessible from the St. Marks Refuge along Live Oak Island Road, at the West Goose Creek Seine Yard and at Wakulla Beach which is at the end of Wakulla Beach Road.

Wakulla Beach Road

Wakulla Beach Road is the first dirt road to the south off U.S. Highway 98 west of the Wakulla River Bridge. The road ends at Wakulla Beach, but it might have been better named Wakulla Salt Marsh. The remnants of an old Hotel sit a few feet back into the vegetation.

You can reach four to six feet of water by wading out from the end of the road. Redfish and speckled trout are plentiful at times. Gander Creek channel flows close to the shoreline to the west. Also, Goose Creek channel which is about 1/4 to a 1/2 mile walk isn't too far away for an energetic wading angler.

Live Oak Island

To reach Live Oak Island turn south off U.S. Highway 98 about five miles west of the Wakulla River onto County Road 365. About a mile and a half south of Highway 98, County Road 367 branches off to the left. Another mile and a half farther County Road 367A again branches off to the left. The road ends at Live Oak Island.

There are spots along the road where the Goose Creek Channel swings close to the shore. Waders can also find water deep enough to hold fish by wading in an easterly direction from Live Oak Point.

Goose Creek Seine Yard

West Goose Creek Seine Yard is located on County Road 367A about two miles from the intersection with County Road 367. There's a dirt road that turns to the left. There are remnants of the watchtower, and other structures once used by mullet fishermen when the seine yard was actively fished.

WADE FISHING TECHNIQUES

Any of the fishing techniques covered in the chapter on Apalachee Bay can be affective in the shallow near-shore waters. Topwater plugs, slow sinking MirrOlures, 1/8-ounce jigs, and shrimp with popping corks are all good choices for speckled trout and Spanish mackerel.

A common approach used on the grass flats throughout Florida is to attach a floating bait bucket full of live shrimp to your belt loop with a fish stringer. This way your bait stays healthy, close-by, and doesn't interfere with your fishing; and you have a place to stringer fish.

Try using light tackle to cast and slowly retrieve a shrimp with a small splitshot. Hook the shrimp just beneath the horn on the top of its head so it pulls straight through the water. Use a slow, "bottom-hopping" retrieve until the pinfish start attacking, then change to a steady retrieve which will allow the bait to last longer.

At the same time, ignore the tapping of the pinfish and wait for the sure hit of a larger fish. Any gamefish "worth its salt" will take notice of the commotion.

CAUTION: Tidal currents can be very strong near the mouth of any of the tidal creeks or coves along the coast. Also, the shoreline east of the lighthouse is closed and protected by the refuge so you have to return to shore at the lighthouse.

We strongly recommend that waders use some kind of foot protection, and know how to swim. Shells, oysters, barnacles, glass, metal objects, crab traps, etc. have a way of finding bare feet and ruining your day — so can a sting ray which might be lying quietly on the sandy bottom until stepped on. Shuffling your feet as you walk will scare them away before you can surprise them.

In addition, when wading out from the lighthouse be wary of boats cutting close to shore on their way into the river. This is a shallow-water shortcut that most boats can only navigate while cruising on a plane. As a result, the boat captains aren't going to want to slow down, so make sure they see you in plenty of time. Boaters, on the other hand, need to realize the affect their wake has on a wading angler who is already standing in four-feet of water.

For boat ramp infomation see pages 112-113. For more information on the St. Marks National Wildlife Refuge call or write to P.O. Box 386, St. Marks, FL 32355; (904) 925-6121; or stop by the visitor center inside the main entrance to the St. Marks Unit of the refuge. To get there turn south on County Road 59, off U.S. Highway 98, just east of the Newport bridge over the St. Marks River.

During spring and fall, gamefish and anglers gather around the mouth of the St. Marks River.

St. Marks River

The Gateway to Apalachee Bay
(*See map page 26*)

The St. Marks River is the most popular access to Apalachee Bay for saltwater anglers in Florida's Big Bend. Supported by the tributary waters of the Wakulla River it's also the largest source of freshwater entering the bay. A lighthouse stands near the entrance to the river, and a Coast Guard navigation channel is marked about six miles upstream to the town of St. Marks.

The St. Marks is a relatively short river that originates in a swampy area east of Tallahassee. On its way to the coast it drops underground at a spot appropriately called Natural Bridge, only to arise a few hundred feet farther to the south. Numerous large and small springs add their waters to the river during its journey.

The Wakulla River joins the St. Marks just below the town of St. Marks at an historically significant site known locally as the Old Fort. Fort San Marcos de Apalache has flown the flags of four governments including Britain, Spain, the Confederacy, and the United States. Today a museum stands on the site.

The river holds the interest of saltwater fishermen from late fall to early spring. That's when fish from the flats invade, often traveling as far upstream as the Highway 98 Bridge at Newport, a distance of about eight miles from the Gulf.

The section from Newport to the Gulf can be characterized as two distinct stream types. From Newport to the town of St. Marks the river winds through a hardwood forest that alternates with sections of low swampy, bottomland. The river channel is deep enough to accomodate medium to small boats as far upstream as the Newport Bridge, which is about all the farther saltwater fish ever travel, and then only during the coldest weeks of the years.

From the town of St. Marks to the Gulf the river flows through a coastal saltmarsh. Below the confluence with the Wakulla River, the St. Marks becomes much wider and oyster bars begin bracketing the channel. The bars become more abundant near the mouth of the river.

Seasons

Every fall sand seatrout, spotted seatrout, redfish, gray snapper, flounder, drum, and sheepshead begin crowding into coastal rivers and creeks. Strictly because of its size, large numbers of these fish head for the St. Marks River.

When the water temperature first begins to drop in September there's an increase in the number of fish around the mouth of the river. For a few weeks they'll move in and out of the freshwater while their bodies go through a process called "osmotic regulation." Essentially they are adjusting to a lower salinity. The procedure is apparently vital. If you put a trout caught on the flats in a livewell and travel upstream it won't survive the change in salinity.

The whole process reverses itself in the spring when the temperature begins to climb and the fish start moving downstream. One of the slowest times of the year can occur when alternating cold and warm fronts start showing up, bouncing the water temperature up and down. For about six weeks, beginning around the first of February and ending near the end of March, fishing becomes a guessing game — how far down the river will the fish be today, or is this the week they return to the flats. If you guess right you can have some big days in the spring, guess wrong and you have to revert to one of those "feel-good" philosophies like "a bad day on the water is better than a good day at the office."

Seatrout and Redfish

Oyster bars, spoil areas, natural rock outcroppings, creek channels, and other "run-outs" are typical places for seatrout and redfish to hangout. There are no end to such areas along both sides of the lower St. Marks. When river fishing, it's important to try different strategies and different locations until you hit upon a combination that's right for that day.

Trolling is one method that will allow you to cover a lot of water while looking for fish. With an electric motor, or small gasoline engine troll slowly up and down the full length of any oyster bars you can get to.

Lure choices are simple. We recommend a 1/4 or 1/2-ounce weedless spoon to help prevent snags on the oyster shells. Other choices include a Texas-rigged, curly-tailed or grub-tailed jig, or a MirrOlure.

In cooler months you can often find "puppy drum" (small redfish) around the spoil islands and along the shoreline of the lower St. Marks River.

Another method is to drift with the tide and/or wind and cast around the oyster bars, around the mouths of tributary creeks and around points along the shoreline. Pay special attention to ends of oyster bars and narrow spots where the current speeds up.

Use the same lures recommended for trolling. Also, any of the new brands of stick lures made by Culprit, BangOlures, and Bomber work well in the shallow water around the oyster bars. Live shrimp, either free-lined, or fished with a popping cork can be very productive at times.

If you find a productive area you can anchor, or get out and fish from a nearby oyster bar. When fishing from a stationary position you can "tight-line" a shrimp in the swift current with a 1/2 ounce egg-sinker.

As you move upstrem from the mouth of the river, the oyster bars get smaller, then gradually disappear. Gamefish structure is replaced by limerock outcroppings and boulders. Fish around the spoil islands, inside and around the numerous creek mouths and around the pilings at the site of the abandoned 19th century town of Port Leon (located about one and a half miles south of the confluence of the St. Marks and the Wakulla rivers).

Over the years we've found East River, Rock Creek and Four Mile Creek to be very productive for redfish and seatrout during the fall.

Another area that sometimes holds fish in the late spring is the confluence of the two rivers. Fish the shallows just outside of the channel and the rocky point extending from the Old Fort.

Above the power plant in the town of St. Marks the river bends and twists all the way to Newport. There are holes up to 20 feet deep in this section of the river. An electronic depth finder is invaluable in locating the holes and schools of fish.

Shrimp and jigs are your best bet in this part of the river. Jigs tipped with pieces of shrimp or Cotee scented artificial baits can be very effective at times.

Shown above are dock pilings at the old site of the 19th century town of Port Leon. The pilings are the remains of a dock that existed when the headquarters of the St. Marks National Wildlife Refuge were located at the old town site. Occasionally, during the cooler months small redfish can be found hanging around the structure and along the shoreline nearby.

Gray (Mangrove) Snapper and Sheepshead

Both mangrove snapper and sheepshead can be caught in the St. Marks River year-round. In the summer, sheepshead are usually plentiful but the number of snapper can vary widely from year to year. During the cooler months however, large numbers of both species move farther upstream.

During warmer months snapper and sheepshead can be caught in the channel and in deep holes outside of the main channel. One of the most popular holes is near Channel Markers 17 and 19 in the lower river. You'll need an ounce or more of weight to hold the bottom if the tide is moving, less if you are using light line in slow water.

Use stiff tackle when bottom fishing and set the hook at the first sign of a nibble. Then replace your bait. Live, or fresh dead shrimp are the best choice for mangrove snapper, and you'll need plenty of it. Fiddler crabs, if you can catch them, are excellent bait for sheepshead.

During the cooler months both species can be caught in the river above the power plant in the town of St. Marks. In general though, only the smaller ones of the species, usually less than 12 inches long, are willing or able to move this far into the freshwater. Larger snapper eventually move away from shore and into deeper water.

When the river is clear you can spot both sheepshead and snapper against the light-

Mangrove snapper are plentiful but small in the St. Marks River.

colored, limestone bottom. The fish prefer deep rocky areas. Try fishing anywhere within a mile or two above the power plant. Pay special attention to the outside of bends in the river where there's a rocky bottom.

Fishing Approach

Once you find fish, anchor upcurrent and cast back to the same area. The rocks make it very difficult to cast and fish upstream.

Snapper often won't take a bait that is acting unusual. Your bait should either lie on the bottom or drift naturally with the current. A bait that is hanging suspended in the current just doesn't look real and won't draw much attention.

Fresh shrimp works best, either whole or broken in pieces. If the fish are actively feeding, use a piece just large enough to surround the hook and enable it to bounce along the bottom.

Use a #1 or smaller hook, and enough weight to take the bait to the bottom in the swift river current. After the bait hits bottom, lift it up a couple feet and let the current take it downstream two or three more feet. Both snapper and sheepshead will be holding directly on the bottom.

When you find an area holding snapper or sheepshead, anchor upstream and fish back to the spot.

Wakulla River

This beautiful southern river is a haven for wildlife and good fishing.

The Wakulla is a broad shallow river that flows between low, swampy banks from its origin in Wakulla Springs to the point where it merges with the St. Marks River about six miles from the Gulf. For saltwater fishermen, the river is really only important during the cooler months when at least a portion of the inland-bound gamefish go left at the juncture of the two rivers. Often, the first sign that saltwater fish have invaded the river is when bass fishermen start catching redfish.

Fishing the Wakulla River for reds and seatrout is a little different than the St. Marks. Eelgrass, hydrilla and other aquatic plants grow so thick throughout most of the river that fishing can be very difficult.

Jigs or shrimp with a popping cork are the easiest choices for fishing openings in the vegetation. Jigs can be rigged Texas-style like you would a plastic worm to help it pull through the weeds. When there is enough open water you can switch to weedless spoons, MirrOlures, live shrimp, or cut bait like strips of mullet or ladyfish.

In general, fish anywhere that you can find something different like a bend in the river channel, a rocky bottom, a deep hole, a log jam, or even a hole in the grass. Use a depth finder if you have one. Also, fish the edge of the main channel and any ledges that you can find.

The water is so clear that you can often see pods of redfish on the bottom. Sometimes the water seems to actually take on the bronze color of these popular fish. Stay ready with a rigged bait or lure for quick action any time you spot fish.

Saltwater gamefish seldom travel farther up river than the bridge at U.S. Highway 98, although an occasional redfish will venture a little farther.

Fishing in the "basin" where the St. Marks and Wakulla Rivers merge can sometimes produce big catches of seatrout and redfish in the fall and

The site of Fort San Marcos de Apalache at the confluence of the St. Marks and Wakulla rivers is a popular fishing spot.

early winter. There is a sand bar on the south side of the St. Marks River. Try trolling or drifting and casting all along the edge of the dropoff.

On the inside of the confluence of the two rivers, at the site of Fort San Marcos de Apalache, a point of land juts out into the river that is only exposed at extremely low tides. If you hit it at the right time you can find seatrout, redfish, sand trout, sheepshead, black drum, and ladyfish where the bottom drops off into deeper water.

About a mile and a quarter up the Wakulla River from the point where it joins the St. Marks is Big Boggy Creek which branches off the east side of the river and runs almost to Highway 98. When seatrout and redfish are in the river they can sometimes be found hanging around the mouth of the creek.

A little farther up the river on the left, are the remnants of an old dock which sometimes attract seatrout and redfish.

Tidal Creeks

More Than Just A Pretty Place

In years past, coastal tidal creeks in the Big Bend area were largely the domain of the small john boat and mullet fisherman's tunnel boat. However, an increase in the use of shallow running boats, and an increased interest in shallow-water fishing brought about by a resurgence of redfish populations, has introduced many anglers to the fine fishing and enjoyable scenery the coastal creeks have always harbored.

In winter, common loons, American mergansers, and a variety of migrating waterfowl use these isolated waterways. Wading birds hunt in shallow water along the shoreline and occasionally you'll see a rail venture out of the marsh grass next to the water.

It's also not unusual to see porpoise crashing against the shoreline pinning mullet in the shallows, while a few yards upstream, an alligator might slide into the water at the boat's approach.

There are dozens of creeks to choose from. A few have freshwater origins from either runoff or springs, but most are tidal streams that branch into smaller and smaller streams that eventually end (or begin) in the salt marsh.

Many of the creeks are guarded by sandbars and oyster bars. The most treacherous and feared of the creek sentinels, however, are limestone boulders and outcroppings.

Many saltwater creeks branch off directly from local rivers like the St. Marks and Aucilla. Creeks near the mouth of a river often have oyster bars near the entrance or just inside. In most cases, there's a natural channel leading around, or through the bars if you can find it. We recommend small to middle size boats for the smaller creeks. Boats and canoes that can be dragged or pushed over bars and rocks are ideal. Boats over 18 feet in length will find the maneuvering difficult in all but the larger creeks.

Some creeks can only be entered during a rising tide and you have to leave when the water does. In other creeks you can enter prior to the falling tide and fish the remaining deeper areas until the tide returns.

The wind can also be a factor. An onshore wind can hold water in the creeks longer, or create "fishable" water levels in the creeks earlier in the tide.

It is possible to get stranded between tides in some of these creeks. Be aware of the tides, and the wind, and plan to leave while there is still plenty of water for your boat at the mouth of the creek — not where you happen to be fishing. If you're going to go exploring, carry extra water, food, clothing, and a can of bug spray regardless of the time of year; and always carry a chart.

Tidal Creeks East of the St. Marks River

Tidal creeks that extend inland from Apalachee Bay are often rocky, especially near their entrances. This is particularly true of creeks between the St. Marks and Econfina Rivers.

One approach is to carefully scout the area as much as possible during the low tide. Learn the location of the obstructions so you can maneuver safely during high tide. If nothing else, seeing what is "down there" can be a long-time reminder of why caution is so important.

There are at least 31 named creeks and maybe half again as many that are unnamed or unmapped. The first four creeks to the east of the lighthouse have a bottom composed primarily of mud, sand, and grass, with a few oyster bars and very little rock. Limerock formations begin to appear near Stony Bayou Creek and continue eastward both in the creeks and along the shore. Depths in most of these creeks vary from very shallow to 10 to 12 feet. Some have palms and cedar trees standing in small clumps along the banks.

Creeks West of the St. Marks River

About 14 creeks extend inland from the West Flats, which is the area of Apalachee Bay extending to the west of the St. Marks River. Some are quite large. Most of these creeks have good depths once you get inside, but their entrances are protected by shallow sandbars and oyster bars. In addition, the shallow grass flats near shore in this part of the bay can be difficult or impossible to cross during low tide.

A description of these creeks, passes, and coves would be generally the same as on the East Flats except there are virtually no rocks to speak of. One exception is in Goose Creek Bay where there are one or two submerged/emerged limestone rock formations and there may be others we are not aware of. Occasional clumps of cabbage palms along the shoreline mark the remnants of ancient barrier islands.

There's also an old creek channel in the bottom of Goose Creek Bay near Live Oak Point in which the water drops off by nine or ten feet. Although we've never caught many fish in the channel itself, the grass flats on both sides can be productive in the summer for seatrout for an hour or two during the rising tide.

One explanation for the pattern would be that while the seatrout aren't feeding they lay in the creek channel where the water is slightly cooler. During the best feeding conditions, when the current is the strongest, they move into the shallow water. In addition, the flats are very shallow in this part of the bay, encouraging larger gamefish to seek deeper water during low tide.

Fishing the points on each side of the opening to a tidal creek can be productive for redfish and seatrout in the spring and fall.

Fishing the Creeks

Typically, gamefish enter the creeks with the rising tide and leave with the falling tide. However, that's not always the case. In some creeks, especially the larger ones, the fish inside the creek will simply gather in deep holes until the water returns.

When the water cools in the fall and on through the spring, numerous species of saltwater fish, including redfish, seatrout, flounder, and sheepshead, crowd into the larger marsh creeks producing some of the best action to be found along the coast.

Creek fishing can be approached much the same as on the flats. Plastic or feathered jigs, MirrOlures, gold spoons, shrimp, and pinfish are all reliable. The only difference is you might find yourself fishing in deeper water than on the flats and need to allow time for jigs or natural baits to reach the bottom.

In small creeks pay particular attention to the outside of bends where you can usually find the deepest water. In larger creeks the deepest water is often near the middle where the current is strongest. In these spots use a 1/2 to 1-ounce sinker to hold the bait in place. If using jigs, switch to 1/2 or 3/4-ounce jig heads.

When you find fish, continue drifting through the same area. Or quietly anchor and work the same spot until the fish quit hitting. In general, you'll do best if you move around a lot and keep looking for fish.

Creek fishing isn't all that productive during the summer, but sometimes redfish, seatrout, tarpon, and even cobia are caught near the mouth of some of the larger creeks. The one exception would be redfish, which can be found well inside the saltmarsh almost anytime of the year.

Redfish

The generally followed redfish pattern is to follow the fish into the creeks as soon as there is sufficient water. Gold spoons will allow you to cover a lot of water with a reliable lure. Stay on the move, fish around the mouths of the creeks and well inside.

A live pinfish free-lined around the oysters bars inside some of the creeks, or anchored with a slipsinker in the current can be very effective, especially in the spring and fall.

Large seatrout can often be found around coastal tidal creeks in the late summer and early fall.

Seatrout

In the fall (September, October, and November), large seatrout can be caught just inside the mouth of some of the larger creeks. If you're willing to spend a few hours working a noisy topwater plug, you're likely to entice a strike or two from one of these "gator" trout. Work the plug along the marshgrass and around any points on the shoreline, much like you would fishing for largemouth bass in the spring.

Use something like a Bomber Rip Shad, or 21M MirrOlure. It's also a good idea to use a monofiliment leader of 25 to 30 pound test for that occasional bluefish that might still be hanging around. If you want to fish with shrimp, use a popping cork and make a lot of noise like you would with a surface plug.

The best conditions for this type of fishing is when there is little or no wind, but the twisting nature of the creeks usually provides for some sheltered water. The quieter the water the farther away the fish will hear the sounds of the lure or popping cork.

Artificial Reefs

Locations and Materials

NAME	DEPTH	LORAN COORDI-NATES	DIS-TANCE FROM SHORE	DATE ESTAB-LISHED	MATERIALS DEPOSITED
ST.MARKS	20	14478.0 46426.0	5.0	1964 1988	TIRES/CULVERTS CULVERTS
ROTARY-Ochlockonee	30	14449.4 46421.0	9.0	1964 1990	TIRES/CULVERTS BRIDGE RUBBLE
OAR/WAKU-LLA-DZ#3*	55	14397.5 46346.8	12	1989 1992	10 MIXERS/115 CUL. 200 CULVERTS
OAR/WAKU-LLA-DZ#1*	55	14394.6 46350.0	12	1990	34 BOATMOLDS & BRIDGE RUBBLE
OAR/CARR-ABELLE	35	14353.4 46475.7	3.0	1992	200 CULVERTS
"ONE MORE TIME"SITE	40	14331.4 46470.0	4.9	1992	75 FT. STEEL HULL SHRIMPBOAT
NEW SITE	75	14313.5 46364.6	12	-----	NO MATERIALS YET

Largely through the activities of the <u>Organization for Artificial Reefs</u>, a Tallahassee-based organization, the nearshore waters of Florida's Big Bend have a number of artificial reefs for the sports angler to choose from. OAR uses donated material along with funds from organization activities and grants to create the artificial habitats.

Artificial Reefs

OAR/Wakulla Artificial Reef

The OAR/Wakulla Artificial Reef consists so far of two separate drop sites. Material was first placed at Drop Zone Number 3 (DZ #3) in 1989. It consisted of 10 cement mixers and 115 concrete culverts. In 1992, 200 more concrete culverts were added to the same site.

In 1990, 34 concrete boat molds along with a portion of the rubble of the old Walker Bridge over the Ochlockonee River was delivered to Drop Site Number 1 (DZ #1).

Fishing

The reef is located in 55 feet of water and is well on its way to establishing a thriving habitat. Because of the depth, bottom fishing will bring the best results. Squid, cigar minnows, pinfish, alewives, and cut mullet will all catch fish. Sea bass, grouper, king mackerel, and sharks have all taken up permanent or seasonal residence on the structure.

If you're intent on trolling then you can expect to catch king or Spanish mackerel. Try spoons or dusters and use downriggers or deep trolling planers to get the baits down near the structure.

Location

The reef is located about 12 miles south of the mouth of the Ochlockonee River. Loran Coordinates for DZ #1 are 14394.6/46350.0; and for DZ #3 are (14397.5/46346.8). DZ #3 is also marked by a yellow and blue buoy.

The Organization for Artificial Reefs and Wakulla County prepared and sank a DC-3 on the Ochlockonee/Rotary Artificial Reef in the summer of 1988.

Ochlockonee/Rotary Artificial Reef

Material was first deposited at the site of this artificial reef in the 1960s. In the summer of 1988 the reef was enlarged and rejuvenated with assorted concrete culverts and steel rubble that was arranged along a 1000 foot north/south axis in 20 to 30 feet of water.

The fuselage of a WW II vintage DC-3 cargo plane was also dropped on the site, as were sections of the Walker Bridge, which spanned the Ochlockonee River at U.S. Highway 98 for 53 years before being dismantled and turned into bottom habitat.

Members of OAR supervised the placement of material on the reef in a manner that would be most productive as fish habitat. For example, a piece of culvert standing on end won't attract as many fish as when it's lying on its side.

A buoy marking the reef is maintained by OAR.

Fishing

The whole range of pelagic bottom fish can be caught at the Ochlockonee Reef: sea bass, Key West grunts, triggerfish, cobia, flounder, grouper, jewfish, king mackerel, Spanish mackerel, and sharks. Divers have reported seeing large gag grouper and jewfish inhabiting some of the large culverts.

Flounder fishing can be exceptional on the reef. The "door mats" like to lie in ambush on the sandy bottom near the structure. Live chubs, rigged with a one-ounce egg-sinker and about 15 inches of leader are deadly. Drop the bait to the bottom and let it swim a few feet away from the sinker.

If you start losing too many baits to grunts and sea bass, you can try jigging for the flounder with four inch strips of cut bait. Cut the strips from mullet or pinfish.

Live pinfish are excellent baits for grouper. It's easy enough to pick up a couple dozen on the flats on the way out to the reef. Pinfish should be fished directly on the structure. Grouper are more plentiful on this shallow-water reef during the cooler months.

King mackerel and Spanish mackerel are also attracted to the waters near the reef. The mackerel fishing is particularly good in the spring, (April, May, and early June). For Spanish mackerel troll silver spoons in the one-half to one ounce range; use larger spoons for the kings. For both species troll back and forth over and along the reef.

Sea bass can be caught on the structure any time of the year. They'll hit jigs, spoons, or chunks of cut bait. When bait fishing, use a smaller hook, or small jigs to catch more fish. Work the baits and lures slowly along the bottom.

To catch a variety of fish, try trolling with large spoons, dusters or jigs (either with of without natural bait trailers).

Drifting across the reef can also be productive. Cast with artificial lures or fish on the bottom with natural bait. If the tidal current or wind is too strong try anchoring upcurrent and drifting bait back to the structure.

Lures and baits
Captain Action spoons, Clark spoons, or Reflecto spoons in either silver or banana color have been productive on the reef. MirrOlures, yellow or white dusters, jigs, and crankbaits are also good at times. For natural baits use squid, cigar minnows, herring, alewives, pinfish and shrimp.

Location:
The reef is located 7.2 miles from the Number 1 Sea Buoy out of St. Marks on a heading of 197 degrees, or approximately 9 miles from Shell Point on a heading of 158 degrees.

Loran C Coordinates for the north end of the reef are 14450.7/46420.8 and for the south end are 14449.1/46420.8.

St. Marks Artificial Reef

The St. Marks Artificial Reef was first established in the 1960s by volunteer fishermen who deposited steel rubble and tires at the site. It was later rejuvenated in 1988 with concrete rubble deposited by the Organization for Artificial Reefs (OAR).

The reef material, which sits in 18 to 20 feet of water, is arranged in roughly a circular pattern. It sits on a sandy bottom dotted with occasional patches of seagrass.

Perhaps the reef's greatest attraction, however, is its proximity to safe harbor. Less than four miles from the mouth of the St. Marks River, it's close enough to shore for small boats to take advantage of reef fishing, and still duck quickly into safe port in case of a change in the weather.

Black sea bass, Key West grunts, triggerfish, squirrelfish, cobia, gag grouper, Spanish mackerel, and sharks are seasonal or year-round residents on the St. Marks Reef.

Bouy are regularly placed to mark the various artificial reefs.

Trolling

You can take a general approach to fishing the reef about anytime of the year by trolling spoons, plugs, or jigs. With this approach you can expect to catch about anything but sharks, while at the same time locating the hottest spots. Troll deeper during the winter months for grouper and black sea bass. During the warmer months troll closer to the surface for Spanish mackerel and king mackerel.

Try trolling with silver or chartreuse spoons, sinking MirrOlures, white, yellow or chartreuse crankbaits, and yellow or white dusters.

Use 40 to 60 pound test monofilament for a leader and attach it with a barrel swivel to keep the line from twisting.

Bottom Fishing

Drifting or anchoring while bouncing natural baits on the bottom is a reliable way to catch fish, especially sea bass and grunts. During the colder months, usually January, February, and March, black sea bass and grouper move closer to shore providing small boat owners who pick a good day a chance to try some bottom fishing normally reserved for areas much farther offshore.

Live bait can be very effective. Use live pinfish, cigar minnows, or a small sea bass you might happen to catch. Cut or whole dead baits can include cigar minnows, squid, alewives, shrimp, cut mullet, pinfish, sardines, and menhaden. Use a Number 8/0 or 9/0 hook for grouper and a much smaller Number 1/0 or 2/0 if your target is sea bass, grunts, or triggerfish.

Cobia

The St. Marks Reef is too close to shore to draw any truely big grouper, but it makes up for it with its ability to attract cobia.

During the warmer months, these powerful gamefish gather around the reef's structure. Live baits free-lined over the reef or suspended three to five feet below a large bobber are great ways to get their attention. Use pinfish or cigar minnows and hook the baits just beneath the dorsal fins with a number 8/0 hook and 40 to 60 pound test leader.

Cobia can also be caught on large feathers. Try chartreuse or white in the 3/4 to 1-ounce size depending on the depth of water and how hard the tide is running. You'll have better luck with feathers when looking for cobia around buoys and pilings. (See section on Cobia fishing.)

Remember, when you hook a cobia, check the water for a second fish trailing around with the hooked fish. The trailing fish, perhaps thinking it's missing out on a meal, can often be enticed to take a well-placed bait or feather.

Location

The reef is 1.9 nautical miles, on a heading of 139 degrees from the Number One Sea Buoy marking the beginning of the St. Marks Channel. A buoy marks the location of the reef, however, the buoy breaks free or disappears from time to time and has to be replaced; so there is no guarantee the reef will be marked.

Loran C Coordinates are 14478.3/46426.5.

Concrete rubble and mixing drums have been deposited on many area reefs.

Spotted seatrout are by-far the most sought after gamefish in the Big Bend area.

Spotted Seatrout

Cynoscion nebulosus

Plain and simple, the Big Bend coast is spotted seatrout country. A vast carpet of turtle grass, eelgrass, and manatee grass extends from the shoreline for many miles offshore—ideal habitat for seatrout and seatrout fishermen.

Also called spotted weakfish, speckled trout, gator trout, winter trout, and saltwater trout, the spotted seatrout is Florida's most popular saltwater gamefish. They are dark gray on the back changing to silvery below. An uneven pattern of black spots completes their decorations.

The largest seatrout ever caught in Florida weighed 15 lbs. 8 ozs., which is 10 ounces lighter than the world record. The average weight normally caught by hook and line anglers is about one and a half pounds.

Spotted seatrout spawn in high salinity areas of bays and sounds, and in shallow areas around barrier islands. Spawning begins in mid-spring and continues to early fall. Females of the species usually outlive the males and grow to a much larger size.

Seasons

Seatrout first begin to show up on the flats in the spring when the water temperature reaches about 68 degrees and holds there for a few days. They stay on the flats until fall when the temperature again drops into the 60's.

Sometime during September, trout move into tidal creeks and tributaries that empty directly into the flats or into one of the local rivers. As the water temperature continues to fall, they move farther up the river in search of food and warmer water. Large trout don't migrate as far up-river as smaller fish but instead hang-out in the deeper holes closer to the coast.

Around the end of December and throughout January trout can be hard to find. If you do happen to locate any, they're usually very sluggish and slow to hit. About mid-March, they again return to the flats and the cycle starts once again.

Bait and Tackle

Medium-sized spinning outfits are probably the most commonly used seatrout tackle, but about anything will let you bring fish to the boat including spinning reels, bait-casting reels, and flyrods.

Artificial lures which have lots of flash are recommended for seatrout. MirrOlures, Bombers, Rebels, Bang-O-Lures, and Rat-L-Traps are all good. ·

Most flats fishermen, however, prefer fishing with some brand of lead-headed jig. Almost any color or style will work, but vary them until you hit a color that works best in the water clarity you're fishing in.

Leader material should be at least 14 to 20 pound test monofilament or steel. In clear water use a light leader, or none at all.

Natural baits for trout include shrimp, pinfish, alewives, clams, small crabs, squid, eels and cut mullet. The baits are best used with a popping cork and a 1/0 or 2/0 hook.

The cork should be placed anywhere from 3 feet to 5 feet above the hook. Every few seconds pop the cork with swift jerks of the rod tip. Spotted seatrout are a bottom dwelling fish, spending much of their time down in the grass. But they will feed at any level and will investigate disturbances on the surface.

The nemesis of the shrimp angler are the hordes of pinfish that inhabit the seagrass. Before you get too mad about them stealing your bait, consider the fact that if you don't have baitfish around, you won't have trout around either. Instead, turn it to your advantage, every time you catch a small pinfish use it for bait, chances are you won't be disappointed. (For more information on catching trout with pinfish see the chapter on Keaton Beach).

When you hook a seatrout, bring it slowly and steadily to the boat, a hurried retrieve can tear their soft mouth. When planning to release a seatrout, try not to remove it from the water. Handle it as little as possible, and do so with wet hands. If a fish becomes stressed and struggles to stay upright, hold it in the water and move it slowly back and forth forcing water over its gills until it recovers.

When a small pinfish steals your shrimp, turn the tables and put it back out as bait. You won't be disappointed.

Drifting the Flats

Casting and drifting is the best way to locate feeding trout on the flats. During April and May begin fishing in 6 to 8 feet of water and continue working your way gradually towards shore. When the trout first hit the flats, they usually gather near shore and not too far from the rivers. Later in the summer concentrate your efforts on areas that have the thickest, healthiest expanses of seagrass.

The best way to fish the flats is to look for structure. That doesn't mean looking for tree trunks or sunken ships. But always look for something to aim your cast at. A clump of weeds, a patch of open bottom, the edge of a sandbar or creek channel, a rock outcropping, or any disturbance on the surface, no matter how slight.

On windy days or when the tide is running strong, you can work hard against the current or fish a method called dropping back. Put out a shrimp without a bobber and a small split shot. Let it fall behind the boat.

With the bail open on a spinning rod, stop the line with your hand. The motion of the boat will tighten the line and swing the shrimp up off the bottom. This is when most hits occur. By holding the line in your hand, when you feel a strike you'll be able to drop out a couple of feet of slack line while you get in position to set the hook.

If the shrimp reaches the surface unmolested, quickly pull out a few more feet of slack line, let the shrimp fall back into the grass, and start the process over.

When you catch the first trout, toss out a marker buoy so you can swing around and repeat the same drift. Where there's one trout, there's bound to be more.

Shallow-Water Seatrout

Every summer, beginning as early as mid-July and continuing through August, large seatrout seem to move into the shallows near shore. The marsh edges and small creeks west of the St. Marks Lighthouse is an area that produces a few of these "gator" trout every year.

Fish with topwater plugs like a Rip Shad, Devil's Horse, MirrOlure or Bang-O-Lure. Use a trolling motor or the current and wind to move along within casting distance of the shore. Also work back into the small bays and a short distance into any creeks along the shore. Always cast to any points of land and cast close to the shoreline.

The key here is diligence and patience. The big trout are there but they're not likely to be present in large numbers. Plan a full day and keep fishing. When that incredible topwater explosion occurs you'll realize a sufficient reward for your patience. A four-pound trout smashing a surface plug is a whole different experience from one-pounders that are quick to suck down a shrimp. If you fish the same waters with jigs, you'll catch small trout, bluefish and flounder, but with the topwater plug you stand a much better chance of finding the big ones.

This is also a good time and place for fly fishermen to tangle with a truly big trout. We recommend medium to large poppers in bright orange or chartreuse colors.

Catching seatrout on topwater plugs can sometimes require a lot of patience, but the returns are often well worth the effort.

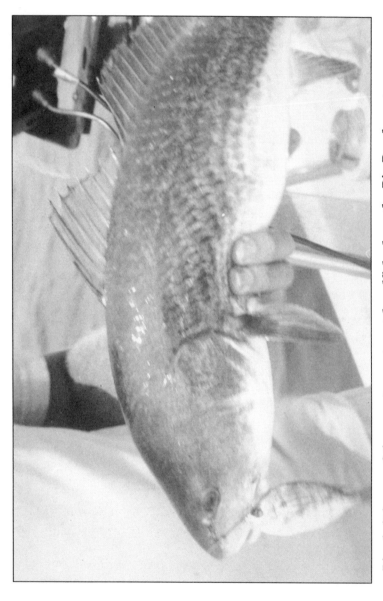

Live bait is one of the surest ways to catch redfish along the Big Bend coast.

Redfish

Sciaenops ocellata

More accurately known as red drum the mighty redfish occurs along the Atlantic coast from Massachusetts to Texas. The largest redfish on record weighed 83 pounds, although fish over 50 pounds are rare.

There's something almost mysterious about these beautiful, silver and coppery hued gamefish that add so much to the excitement of fishing along the Big Bend coast. Few other gamefish contain the same combination of aggressiveness, reliability, and fighting strength.

No matter how many times you experience it, it's always a thrill to feel the familiar pull of a redfish. They have a distinctive, tough-minded way of fighting, and a strength that far exceeds their size. And when you use a shallow-water playing field decorated with sharp edged rocks or oyster bars you're in for a respectable contest.

Redfish prefer rocky areas, oyster bars, mudflats, creek channels, inlets, dock pilings, and jetties. About the only place you don't find them is out on the offshore grassflats, and even that's not unheard of.

Bait and Tackle

Medium-sized spinning or baitcasting rigs will do fine for redfish. Twelve to 14-pound test is sufficient, with a leader of about 25 to 30-pound test monofilament.

A gold spoon is probably the most reliable, all-around lure for catching redfish. We've seldom encountered a time when they obviously preferred some other type of lure over a spoon.

Large plastic jigs are a reliable second choice, however, they're less effective when fishing in shallow, rock-strewn water. With a spoon you can work the lure just above the rocks while covering a lot more water. Other lure choices would include a topwater MirrOlure or one of the new plastic stick baits worked in a zig-zag pattern on or just under the surface.

Flyfishing for redfish is a steadily growing sport in the Big Bend area. Anglers will need at least a number eight or nine rod. A weightforward, floating flyline is a good choice because of the one to three-foot depths you're often fishing in and the difficulty of recovering your line on a back cast. In the Big Bend, flyfishermen prefer gold streamers like Seducers or Deceivers.

Livebait really brings out the aggressive nature of the redfish. We've watched them literally shoulder each other out of the way to get to a struggling baitfish. Pinfish (shiners) are an excellent live-bait choice, followed by mullet and live shrimp. In creeks and rocky areas use a bobber and let the bait drift with whatever current is around. When fishing around jetties, pilings or in deep holes fish on the bottom with a slip-sinker that will give the bait freedom to move while holding it to a relatively confined area.

Seasons

Redfish are creatures of habit. They like to fish at the same time, on the same tide, season after season, and that fact alone can be relied upon to increase your chances of regularly tangling with one. Some of the most reliable redfish haunts in the warmer months along the Big Bend coast are the rocky areas along the shoreline between Stony Bayou Creek and the Aucilla River.

If you've got the nerve, and the patience to explore these booby-trapped areas, you can often find redfish waiting to burst into action. (See the section on Rocks Along the Coast in the chapter on Apalachee Bay for more information on fishing these areas.)

During the winter, turn your attention to the St. Marks, Aucilla and Ochlockonee Rivers. The more severe the winter the farther upstream the fish will move. In the St. Marks they will travel seven or eight miles upstream taking advantage of the even temperatures of the spring-fed waters.

During the fall and spring, look for reds to be active around the numerous creek mouths along the Big Bend coast. The creeks along the coastline north and south of Steinhatchee, in particular, hold some excellent redfish fishing.

When the tide waters start running into the creeks, so do the reds. Fish just inside the mouth of the creek and a couple hundred yards upstream. Concentrate your fishing to times when the current is strongest. Redfish

Regardless of the time of year, oyster bars are popular redfish haunts. In general, fish over the bars at high tide and in the deeper areas between bars at low tide. When the tide is running strong, (which is the best time to fish) pay special attention to spots where the water, and available bait, is squeezed between bars. The bottom line, however, is that any oyster bar, at any time or tide, is worth a cast or two.

can be slow to bite during slack tide. (See the chapter on Steinhatchee for more information on this type of fishing.)

Where Else to Look

There are numerous scattered oyster bars around the mouth of the Ochlockonee River. At high tide, redfish will roam across the bars, searching for food along the bottom. At low tide, look for reds where the tidal flow is squeezed between two emerging bars, or where the current sweeps around the end of a bar.

Farther upriver are a number of creeks that attract redfish in the winter. In general they move into the creeks with the rising tide and out with the falling tide. Because creeks vary in size and depth, redfish may choose different times to enter or leave different creeks.

The lower St. Marks River has a superb network of oyster bars. With an electric trolling motor and a little maneuvering, you can drift through the exposed bars west of the channel looking for reds. Cast well ahead of the boat in the clear shallow water. Work the lure along the edges of the exposed bars and around any points and channels in-between the bars.

There's another nice set of oyster bars in the East River that can be fished the same way. The East River joins the St. Marks just above the lighthouse.

A couple of other well-known redfish spots in the St. Marks River are the boulder strewn border of the spoil island east of the channel about a mile above the lighthouse, and the dock pilings at the old townsite of Port Leon, about a mile below the confluence of the Wakulla and St. Marks Rivers. There's also a number of small creeks leading off the lower St. Marks and East Rivers that attract a fair amount of reds.

In the lower Aucilla River redfish hang around the rocky shelves and limestone outcroppings which are about everywhere. A well-known winter hot spot is a deep hole in the river on the east side of the island that divides the river just below the boat ramp on the lower Aucilla.

Sight Fishing

As a bonus to this nicely packaged gamefish, redfish can often be spotted and cast directly to. Of course, the best viewing station is from a poling platform mounted above a high-tech flats boat. But they can also be spotted from a lower position if the sun is right and the water is clear. Once you catch a glimpse of a school of reds, it's simply a matter of hitting them with a cast before the boat scares them away.

You can also sometimes discover reds "tailing" in shallow water or in the clumps of sargasso-like seaweed that grow along the rocky coastline. Redfish "tail" when grubbing on a muddy bottom or over an oyster bar looking for food. You can actually see their tails sticking out of the water when they poke their noses into the bottom.

Trolling for reds

Trolling is still another method that can be effective. Troll the lures along oyster bars and in the "run-out" channels that form with the tide between oyster bars and spoil areas. An electric trolling motor or a small outboard motor are best to use. Either one will allow you to maneuver close to or even over the oyster bars.

It's also a good idea to troll along the upcurrent side of an oyster bar so the tide will push your lure closer to the structure and away from a direct line behind the boat.

Lure choices for trolling include gold or silver Johnson spoons, Daredevil spoons, Little Cleo spoons, shallow-running MirrOlures, jigs with a curly-tail or grub tail and 1/4-ounce Rat-L-Traps.

Use at least two feet of 25 to 30-pound monofilament leader to avoid cutoffs against rocks or oyster bars.

[For more information on redfish in the Big Bend area see the chapters on Ochlockonee Bay, Steinhatchee and Apalachee Bay.]

This cobia showed up at the boat on a slow afternoon in Apalachee Bay and fell prey to a well-aimed plastic jig.

Cobia

Rachycentron canadum

Also known as lemonfish, ling, sergeant fish, crab-eater, and cabio; cobia are shadowy, stalking, curious fish that can show up anywhere along the Big Bend coast. Common from Argentina to Massachusetts they first appear in the area when the water temperature reaches about 70 degrees and they stay until the same temperature range is reached in the fall.

The world record is currently 135 lbs. 9 ozs. The Florida record is 103 lbs. 12 ozs. Along the Big Bend coast they commonly range from 5 to 50 pounds, with an occasional trophy fish showing up.

Their coloration is quite striking. A dark, chocolate-brown colored back blends into lighter-colored sides with alternating horizontal stripes of brown and silver or bronze and white.

The overall appearance of a cobia is similar to that of a small shark, especially in the water. They also look like big remora without the sucker pad on top. Some anglers feel they resemble a large catfish.

A free-roaming fish, cobia seem to have two things in mind, eating and looking for structure. They surprise grouper fishermen bottom-bouncing in 80 feet of water and trout fishermen jigging in three feet of water. Their habit of swimming near the surface creates an occasional opportunity for sight casting.

Cobia sometimes cooperate by coming right up to a drifting boat. If you're ready with a jig or feather, and can make a cast in the general vicinity of a moving target, you'll be in for a serious thrill.

Cobia Hunting

Of course you don't have to just wait for a cobia to show up at your boat. Instead, you can go looking for them.

Cobia like shade, especially when the sun is high, which might be why they come to a drifting boat. They'll also take up stations next to pilings, buoys, and floating debris. In addition, they'll gather around wrecks, reefs, artificial reefs, and drop-offs.

In Apalachee Bay, look for cobia around the channel markers of the St. Marks Ship Channel and the pilings of the Stake Line, which mark the southern boundary of the St. Marks National Wildlife Refuge. In the ship channel start at Marker 26 and work your way out.

The "Range Finder" (the big tower next to the St. Marks Ship Channel about two miles out from the mouth of the river) can be especially productive for cobia in the summer. You'll have a much better chance of finding cobia there if you can fish on a weekday when there's little or no boat traffic in the channel.

If your boat is large enough, you can fish for cobia at the St. Marks and Ochlockonee Artificial Reefs and Ochlockonee Shoals. (See pages 70, 110 &111 for more information about the reefs.) At the reefs anchor upcurrent and drift a pinfish suspended below a bobber across the structure.

If there's no action for a few minutes, try another spot. If there's a cobia around it will waste little time in finding the bait. Wherever they are, they're seldom so docile that they won't at least investigate about anything that remotely resembles food, even if they choose to swim away.

The best cobia fishing takes place on clear, sunny days with little wind and calm water. The black and white fish are easy to spot under these conditions and they're more likely to be looking for a shady spot. When the water is rough, or the weather cloudy and rainy, the fish are more likely to be scattered, and difficult to spot.

Cobia Spot Fishing

Locating cobia is half the battle, after that it takes a well-placed cast. When fishing around pilings, take a cast before you get close enough to see the fish. You'll run far less risk of scaring them off before hooking one.

Also approach pilings in a direction that doesn't cast a shadow ahead of the boat. Cast a feather or large plastic jig past the piling and work it back through the shadow where the fish will be laying.

Another option is to toss a live pinfish within a few feet of the structure and wait for any lurking cobia to find it. You won't have to wait long.

If you're drifting the flats fishing for seatrout, it's not a bad idea to drift a pinfish behind the boat. Use a bobber set about three feet above the hook, 30 to 50 pound monofilament leader, and 17-pound test line for this type of cobia fishing.

If you see a cobia around the boat, reel the pinfish in close without making too much noise and wait for the visiting fish to notice it. Or if you have time, grab that ready-rigged outfit you always have at hand and drop a lure in front of the fish before it swims on. A large feather or plastic jig will do the trick. Retrieve it fast past the fish, then slow down or stop the lure before it gets to the boat. Don't take it out of the water too soon, a looming boat shadow doesn't bother a cobia when it's chasing a lure.

Locations and Loran Numbers
These are some of the places you should visit if you go on a cobia hunting tour of Apalachee Bay.

1. Channel Markers denoting the St. Marks Ship Channel from Marker Number 26 to Number 1 Sea Buoy.

2. "Stake Line" pilings marking the boundary of the St. Marks National Wildlife Refuge.

3. Sunken Barge located at 14441.7/46346.4.

4. St. Marks Artificial Reef—1.9 nautical miles, on a heading of 139 degrees from the Number One Sea Buoy marking the beginning of the St. Marks Channel. A buoy sometimes marks the location of the reef, however, it disappears from time to time so there is no guarantee the reef will be marked. Loran C Coordinates are 14478.3/46426.5.

5. Ochlockonee Artificial Reef located 7.2 miles from the Number One Sea Buoy out of St. Marks on a heading of 197 degrees, or approximately 9 miles from Shell Point on a heading of 158 degrees. Loran C Coordinates for the north end of the reef are 14450.7/46420.8 and for the south end are 14449.1/46420.8. (See page 70 for more on the reefs.)

6. Bell Buoy Number 24 — an intracoastal channel marker. Eleven miles from Number One Sea Bouy out of St. Marks on a heading of 176 degress, or approximately 12 1/2 miles from the flashing beacon from Shell Point at a heading of 148 degress, or approximately 11 miles from Ochlockonee Point at a heading of 125 degress. Loran C Coordinates of 14443.5/46362.0

Big Spanish mackerel have been showing up in Big Bend waters in larger and larger numbers. These fish were caught by trolling silver spoons.

Spanish Mackerel

Scomberomorus maculatus

Spanish mackerel are plentiful along the local inshore and offshore waters of the Big Bend coast. But it wasn't always that way. For many years Gulf and Atlantic populations were dramatically reduced due to over-fishing, however, restrictions and quotas were eventually placed on both commercial and recreational fishermen and gradually the stocks rebounded.

The spotted, silver and gray fish first appear in the Big Bend area in the spring when the water temperature rises into the upper 60's. April is usually the hottest month, but vigorous mackerel fishing can start as early as late March and continue through May. In the fall, usually during October and November, they again head for warmer waters.

Fishing

Trolling is by far the most popular method for taking Spanish mackerel, and spoons are the most reliable choice of lure. If the action is slow, try tipping the hook with a strip of mullet or other cut bait.

Trolling speeds for Spanish mackerel should be 5 to 12 knots or better, but be sure the lure stays down. You won't be out-running any mackerel, and the fast moving lure will be more natural looking and enticing.

Concentrate your trolling near areas likely to attract mackerel. That especially includes the passes west of the Big Bend area between the barrier islands of Dog Island, St. George Island, Cape St. George, and St. Vincent Island. Troll along the ends of the islands where the bottom drops off, and along sandy spits that protrude into the passes.

Another good spot, that should be fished at low tide is the St. Marks Ship Channel near the mouth of the river. Also, look for Spanish mackerel both north and south of channel markers 5, 6 and 8 where there are shallow sand reefs. Mackerel favor dropoffs, even though the increase in depth may be only three or four feet.

If you troll two lures, run one shallow and the other one deep. If you have mismatched tackle, use a shorter rod on the shallow lure to help it stay at least a few inches under the surface. A longer rod can better handle a small planer or trolling weight that will help keep the lure down.

By keeping the deep-running lure close to the boat, it'll be easier to turn sharply when following irregular grassbeds or sandy stretches. The shallow line can pass over the top of the deeper one. Another option is to run a flatline on each side with a weighted line down the middle.

If there's a chop on the water the spoons on the flat line will often skip and bounce through the waves, which is a good way to attract larger mackerel. On a calm day, it's better to run the flatline a little under the surface.

After their springtime feeding frenzy, Spanish mackerel seem to settle into a steady crusade to rid the Gulf of small fish. At the same time they become a little more discerning while working on one school of baitfish at a time.

For instance, you can troll through a school of glass minnows being harassed by a horde of mackerel and not get a strike because your spoon is larger than the minnows. If you're sure there are mackerel around, keep switching to a smaller and smaller lure until they start to notice.

If necessary, go as small as crappie-sized jigs for trolling or casting. Look for jigs that have strong hooks, mackerel will crush thin hooks or weak-bodied jigs.

Anytime you're out on the water in the summer, keep a sharp look-out for birds wheeling and diving on schools of baitfish. Chances are Spanish mackerel are pushing the baitfish to the surface. If you get there in time, you can take advantage of the situation.

When chasing mackerel in this manner, use light-weight spinning tackle and as light as eight-pound test in order to reach the fish without getting too close with the boat. If possible, position yourself ahead of the school and let them come to you. When the school dives, be patient and watch the birds for a clue as to where the fish will surface again. When a gull or tern drops towards the water, the mackerel may already be on their way back up.

Bait and Tackle

The same small to medium sized rods and reels used for seatrout are fine for catching Spanish mackerel. Some anglers prefer to use a little heavier tackle while trolling.

Either wire, or 50-pound monofilament is a must for leader material. Use a black swivel to connect the line to the leader. In the midst of the action a silver swivel will present a tempting target and can quickly result in a cleanly clipped line. When trolling a spoon use a ball bearing swivel to battle line twists.

Literally dozens of tackle manufacturers make spoons that are effective for casting or trolling including Clark, Captain Action, Drone, and Reflectos. Dusters are also very productive at times, especially when tipped with strips of mullet or ladyfish. Yellow, white, or white/red combinations in feather or nylon material is best. A one or two-ounce trolling sinker, either keel or torpedo style, should be used to keep the lure down. The weight should be placed three to five feet above the end of the line.

Nylure jigs and about any type of plastic jig can be used when casting to mackerel activity. When there's time, tip the hook with small pieces of shrimp or a piece of Cotee's Probait.

During mild winters flounder can be caught around the mouth of the St. Marks River on sandy-bottomed areas between the outer oyster bars.

Flounder

Order Pleuronectiformes

For most area anglers, flounder are a pleasant bonus to a day of fishing for something else. But for some, the tasty fillets are enough incentive to make a special effort to catch them.

Of the more than 200 species of flounder, two are commonly caught by sportfishermen in the waters off the Big Bend coast—the southern flounder (Paralichthys lethostigma) and the Gulf Flounder (Paralichthys albigutta). The southern flounder is the largest and the most common. Both species are white on the bottom and muddy brown to olive on the top. The southern flounder has a scattering of white dots on its dark side and the Gulf flounder has three distinct spots in the shape of a triangle. Both are year-round residents and can be caught in a variety of salinities.

Along the Big Bend, flounder are regularly caught in three feet of water by seatrout fishermen and in 60 feet of water by grouper fishermen. Although they can reach sizes of 20 pounds, locally caught flounder seldom average more than two or three pounds.

Habits

Flounder are among nature's most successful ambushers. They lie in wait disguised as a piece of the bottom until an unsuspecting meal swims by. Then they turn into a piece of bottom with very sharp teeth.

Their flat body design, and ability to match the bottom coloration makes them perfectly adapted for these tactics. On a soft seabed they will even cover themselves with mud or sand. On a hard seabed they simply blend in with the scenery and patiently wait the approach of a careless fish.

As if that weren't enough, they have both eyes on one side of their body, obviously an advantage when most of their time is spent lying on one side looking up. Perhaps even stranger is the fact that they aren't born that way. During a flounder's larval stage one eye actually moves around to the other side of their head. Some flounders end up with both eyes on the left side and some have both eyes on the right. Also, the upper side of the flounder retains the coloration while the bottom side turns white.

Seasons

In the summer months, flounder can be found on sandy or muddy bottoms around the edges of oyster bars, sand reefs, bays, creek mouths, and along shorelines. They also have a tendency to show up in the vicinity of piers and bridges. Tidal rips around creek and river mouths and at the ends of long oyster bars are ideal places to find them. Also, look for depressions or drop-offs near moving water.

Two flounder hot spots during the summer season are the Ochlockonee Artificial Reef and St. Marks Artificial Reef. Another locale often rich with flounder is the outside of the jetties at the Gulf end of Bob Sikes Cut. Baits should be fished close to the structure, and held on the bottom with at least a half-ounce egg sinker.

During late fall, flounder gather at the mouth of the St. Marks River along with redfish and seatrout. They usually hang around the numerous oyster bars and sandbars. When winter settles in, flounder will move upstream, sometimes showing up ten miles from the Gulf.

Bait and Tackle

Young flounder eat small shrimp and other crustaceans. As they grow they graduate to small baitfish including menhaden, mullet, croakers, and pinfish. Live chub minnows, which can be seined or netted near shore also make excellent bait.

Flounder will also hit plastic jigs fished slowly on the bottom. A 6-inch baitstrip attached to the hook will make the lure more attractive. Baitstrips can be made from pinfish, mullet, or squid with the tail split to create a fluttering action. Belly strips from menhaden, herring, porgies, bluefish and shark are also good baits.

Use a plain, straight-shanked hook, (#1, #1/0, or #2/0) with 12 to 18 inches of leader and a 1/4-ounce to 1/2-ounce egg sinker above the swivel. A heavy leader pays off since flounder like to hide around barnacle-covered rocks and other sharp objects.

Fishing Methods

Although very aggressive feeders, flounder don't like to give up their hiding place unless they're sure of a good chance of success. But when a meal does come by within their range of attack they explode from the bottom without hesitation.

Jig fishing for flounder is somewhat akin to largemouth bass fishing with a plastic worm. Work the bait slowly, periodically raising it a few inches then allowing it to drop back to the bottom again. When you feel a strike, resist the urge to set the hook immediately. Instead, count to three, reel in any slack line, and then set the hook hard. Flounder have a small mouth and sometimes take an extra moment to get a firm grip on the bait.

Drift fishing is probably the most effective method since it covers more of the bottom and keeps the bait or lure in motion. Jigs, or sinking MirrOlures are good lure choices when drifting.

Since they spot their prey visually, water clarity is very important. You can expect to catch very few flounder when the water is muddy or stained. Fairly clear water and a rising tide are the best conditions. Fishing should begin as soon as the tide starts in.

If you do manage to catch a couple of these odd-looking creatures, you'll be treated to some of the finest table fare to come out of our local waters. They fillet easily and although the meat from one side is darker than the other, it all tastes good.

There is no bag limit on flounder, but there is an 11-inch size limit.

Gigging

Flounder gigging takes place at night, the darker the better. An ideal time is when there is a high tide just after dark.

The approach is fairly simple, either walk or pole a small boat across a sandy area while searching the bottom with a bright flashlight or Coleman lantern. When you see a flounder, stick it with the gig and put it in the cooler.

Flounder are masters at camouflage, sometimes all you can spot is a faint outline. When that's the case, make sure it isn't a sting ray. They can look very similar when partially covered.

You can keep the sting rays from living up to their names by shuffling your feet when moving around in shallow water. This will scoot the ray out of the way and lessen your chances of being harpooned with a bacteria infected, and barbed, guided missile that seldom misses.

Large male sea bass are sometimes called "humpbacks" because of a protruding lump that forms behind their eyes.

Black Sea Bass

Centropristis striata

Also known locally as rock bass, the black sea bass is sort of the Rodney Dangerfield of bottom fish. They just don't get much respect—especially when they steal a carefully-prepared bait meant for a snapper or grouper. But if you have a boat that can run a few miles offshore, they can be a reliable prey and a good source of protein even though they seldom reach weights of more then one to two pounds.

Sea bass can be an incredibly cooperative fish in the right conditions and seasons. When you "get on 'em," they hit absolutely everything you drop over the side. If you trade the usual bottom-bouncing tackle for a lightweight spinner with 10-pound test and a 1/0 hook, you'll find out just how much fun these aggressive little fish can be.

Sea bass generally inhabit the same types of bottom structure preferred by grouper. It's the nearshore waters, however, from about three to ten miles out that the sea bass have the available structure largely to themselves.

How to find a "SPOT"

Between four and six miles southeast of the mouth of the St. Marks River is some of the best black sea bass fishing in the Gulf of Mexico. In depths ranging from 18 to 22 feet, you can find numerous rocky areas, many with formations projecting upward from the bottom anywhere from one to three feet and some higher.

The bottom structure is home to a variety of marine life that sea bass prey upon. In some areas, coral and manatee grass grows around the rocks.

Trolling is a proven method for locating and catching sea bass if you don't have a Loran unit, or even if you do. One-half to 1-ounce spoons trolled deep will easily attract sea bass. A small planer designed to run to depths of less than twenty feet will increase the lure's effectiveness. In addition to spoons, small crankbaits like a 1/2-ounce Rat-L-Trap or The Spot in silver or gold will also "troll-up" a fishing spot. If the wind will allow, drifting is another good way to locate fish.

As soon as you catch a sea bass, toss out a marker buoy and troll back through the same area or use a depth finder to pinpoint the bottom structure. If you catch another fish drop anchor. When sea bass really start hitting about the only way to stop the action is to keep the lines in the boat.

Bait and Tackle

Use the lightest saltwater tackle you own, or even a retired bass rod. You'll actually catch more fish on light tackle because you'll be able to feel and react to the sharp, short hits.

Sea bass are more aggressive (if that's possible) towards natural baits—shrimp, squid, cigar minnows and pinfish are best. They'll also readily hit jigs and jigs tipped with a piece of natural bait. When the fish gather in large numbers, particularly in the cooler months, they'll hit anything that falls to the bottom. This is a good time to use those beat-up jig heads and off-colored plastic bodies that have been lying in the bottom of your tackle box.

When using a jig, don't exaggerate the action, all you need to do is move the lure along the bottom in little six-inch hops. If the fish are at all plentiful they'll find it before you can move the lure two feet.

If there's much of a tidal current, or you get impatient waiting for the jig to fall to the bottom, put a one-half ounce or larger egg sinker above the swivel.

Seasons

Sea bass can be caught in the same areas year-round, however, January, February and March are the best months. That's when the fish move closer to shore and gather in large numbers. This is also when it's common to catch large males that have developed a protrusive hump on their backs.

Try these places for black sea bass and other bottom fish near shore. All are within 4 to 10 miles of the coast.
St. Marks Artificial Reef 14478.3/46426.5
Ochlockonee/Rotary Artificial Reef 14450.7/46420.8
Sunken barge southeast of buoy #24 14441.7/46346.4
DC-3 Aircraft on Ochlockonee Artificial Reef 14450.3/46422.3
Rock Pile 14475.6/46378.0
Oar/Wakulla Artificial Reef 14393.6/46353.8

Bluefish
Pomatomus saltatrix

The northern Gulf coast doesn't normally see the big schools of large and small bluefish that migrate up and down the east coast of Florida every spring and fall.

The blues that venture into the Big Bend waters are usually small, less than one or two pounds, and they seldom occur in large numbers. It's more common to catch one or two by accident during a whole day of fishing.

Blues are often found traveling with large schools of Spanish mackerel and feeding on the same schools of baitfish. In fact, about the best way to catch a bluefish is to fish for Spanish mackerel; and the best way to find either is to look for a flock of birds feeding on the baitfish scraps floating to the surface near a feeding frenzy.

Bluefish also roam the flats in small numbers ready to strike at any seatrout lure that happens to come their way. Unless you're using a leader, however, you wouldn't even know it was a bluefish that snatched your jig and left you with an empty line to retrieve.

If you do happen upon a few blues, all you need to do is get a lure into the water, preferably one you're not too fond of. When they're "on the feed" these sharp-toothed predators will slash viciously at anything that moves. And again, if you don't use some type of a leader, you might just as well toss the lure in the water without tying it to the line.

Bluefish will also readily hit large chunks of cutbait or belly strips taken from mullet or even a previously caught bluefish.

Also, never use a lure with more than one hook. Multiple hooks won't catch more fish and are incredibly difficult to remove from between all those sharp teeth. The best choice is a Crocodile or other type of silver spoon. They hold up well, cast a long distance, and are easy to disengage from the fishes' teeth. Some east coast fishermen have even been known to replace the treble hook that comes on most spoons with a single hook.

Also, keep your fingers and toes away from the mouth of any bluefish, even when it's in the boat. Bluefish have the ability, rare among fishes, to see well both in and out of the water. They will quickly, and without warning, reach out and take a bite out of any exposed fingers or toes that come within range.

The Year of Big Blues

A few year's ago, a phenomenon occurred along the Big Bend coast, that might only be described as the "Year of the Big Bluefish." For whatever the reason—population boom, food shortage, weather changes—big bluefish, ranging from 10 to 20 pounds, showed up everywhere from the grouper holes offshore to three foot of water on the grassflats.

For about five months they surprised flats fishermen, surf fishermen, and even anglers chasing redfish among the rocks.

If they ever return it might be helpful to know that one of the few places we were able to reliably find big fish was around the shallow sandbars and ridges off the east end of St. George Island on the Gulf side. During high tide that summer they could be seen running back and forth over the sandbars and through the swash channel next to the beach.

If you know there are big bluefish around, try fishing with light tackle, 10 or 12 pound test and about a 25 - 30 pound monofilament leader. Their good eyesight makes the big fish leader-shy, plus when given a chance to run and fight against the light tackle, bluefish put on a gill-flaring, head-shaking, acrobatic display similar to that of largemouth bass.

In return for using a fairly light leader it's important to instantly set the hook at the first sign of a strike. If the fish has a chance to get the lure deep in it's mouth it will be able to sever the monofilament leader. If you set the hook quickly enough to lip-hook the fish, and keep the line tight during the fight, you'll be able to appreciate the accomplishment of landing such a notorious bait-stealer on light tackle.

Sheepshead
Archosargus probatocephalus

Sheepshead are an odd looking fish, with a steep profile and a pointed snout. Their backs and upper sides are a dark olive, and their lower-sides are silvery-colored. Both colors are crossed with a striking pattern of black and white vertical stripes.

Their most outstanding feature, however, and the one for which they are named, is their large, powerful teeth, which protrude like those of a sheep. They have a definite over-bite problem.

Even though sheepshead are one of the most populous fish in the coastal regions of the Gulf of Mexico, they are one of the trickiest fish to catch. The reason is their careful habit of nudging the bait, backing off for a few seconds, then moving back in for a bite. Even then, they'll use their sharp front teeth to clip off small pieces of bait while avoiding the hook.

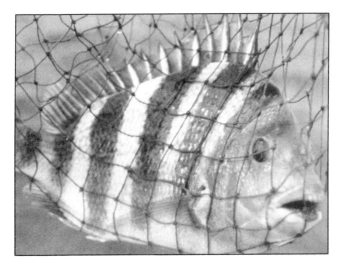

This creates a dilemma for the angler. If you try for a quick set, you'll miss the fish, but if you wait too long you'll soon end up with an empty hook. The old adage says that for sheepshead you have to set the hook right before the fish bites.

Bait and Tackle

Fiddler crabs are by-far the best bait for sheepshead, but since their diet also includes crustaceans and small shellfish, they can be caught on shrimp, clams and oysters.

Sheepshead are normally non-schooling, bottom dwellers, but they do gather in feeding groups around underwater structures such as bridge and dock pilings, where they pick and scrape at barnacles on the structure.

Sheepshead are also known to respond to a chum of ground fiddler crabs mixed with shell and sand. As the sand and shell particles flutter to the bottom with the bits of meat, it imitates debris typically present in the water around actively feeding sheepshead. The chum not only attracts sheepshead, but it also puts them in the mood to grab whole baits instead of just nibbling.

A Few Hot Spots

The St. Marks River produces some excellent catches of sheepshead. Just north of Channel Marker 17, along the western edge of the channel is a good spot. There's also a deep hole near Marker 53 that usually holds sheepshead and other bottom fish. Still another place worth trying is along the edge of the old sunken ship that sits near the lighthouse at the mouth of the river.

During the winter they can be caught in the deep, rocky areas in the river above the town of St. Marks. One good spot is the first sharp bend above the power plant. Most of the fish will run around a half pound or less with an occasional larger fish showing up.

The causeway over to St. George Island is also a good place to fish for sheepshead. Try fishing with fiddler crabs or shrimp on the bottom close to the bridge pilings and along the seawalls. In the fall every year large sheepshead also gather around the jetties of Bob Sikes Cut. Fish off the end of the east jetty with light tackle and whole shrimp. In the swift current you'll have to set the hook very hard at the first sign of a nibble.

Tackle choices are simple, about any rod and reel will do, but a stiffer rod will make it easier to hook the tricky fish. Hooks should be heavy enough to resist being crushed by the strong incisors of a sheepshead, and a short shank will make it easier to penetrate their bony mouths. A good choice is a 2/0 or 3/0 bait hook.

Charts and Maps

For Navigation in the Big Bend Area Use:
United States Coast Guard Chart #11405
Covers Apalachee Bay.
United States Coast Guard Chart #11401
Covers Apalachee Bay to Cape San Blas. Both are available in local tackle stores and marinas.

The Guide to Saltwater Fishing in the Florida Big Bend
A useful chart for locating artificial reefs and other fishing structures — not for navigational purposes. Available at local tackle stores and marinas.

Florida County Maps
A large book of individual county maps in black and white. Each county is on a separate page. Lakes, rivers and boat ramps, major highways and back county roads are noted as well as national forests, recreation areas, wildlife preserves and historical sites. It can be found at many book stores or ordered from the Florida Wildlife Federation, P.O. Box 6870, Tallahassee, FL 32314; (904) 656-7113.

Atlas and Gazetteer
A four-color recreation guide covering the entire state. Contains information on parks, wildlife refuges, campgrounds, fishing, canoe trails, boat ramps, historic sites, recreation areas, and bicycle routes. The Atlas and Gazetteer can be found at many local book stores or ordered from the Florida Wildlife Federation, P.O. Box 6870, Tallahassee, FL 32314; (904) 656-7113.

Loran Coordinates

LORAN NUMBERS AT A GLANCE...Around the Big Bend

Alligator Harbor No. 2..14419.5/46518.4

Bob Sikes Cut...14225.0/46530.0

Dog Island Reef (western end).....................14391.0/46486.0

Fenholloway River...14504.8/46241.6

Intracoastal Waterway Marker No. 18.............14464.1/45994.1

Intracoastal Waterway Marker No. 20.............14479.0/46128.0

Intracoastal Waterway Marker No. 22.............14481.5/46245.5

Intracoastal Waterway Marker No. 24.*...........14443.5/46362.0

Intracoastal Waterway Marker No. 26.**...............14404.9/46407.0

Keaton Beach..14489.1/46076.3

OAR/Wakulla Artificial Reef (drop zone 1).......14394.6/46350.0

OAR/Wakulla Artificial Reef (drop zone 2).......14393.6/46353.4

OAR/Carrabelle Artificial Reef.......................14353.4/46475.7

Ochlockonee Shoals (center)............................14450/46400

* #24 is located near the south end of the Ochlockonee Shoals

** #26 marks the south end of the South Shoals

Loran Coordinates

Ochlockonee Bay Light No. 2......................14444.3/46459.0

One More Time (sunken boat).........................14331.4/46470.0

Rock Pile...14475.6/46378.0

Rotary/Ochlockonee Artificial Reef..............14449.4/46421.0

Steinhatchee Artificial Reef.........................14459.7/46011.3

Steinhatchee No. 1.....................................14472.3/45924.4

Shell Point Light...14470.7/46511.0

Shell Point Marina.......................................14473.5/46512.3

St. Marks Artificial Reef...............................14478.0/46426.0

St. Marks Lighthouse...................................14490.2/46475.8

St. Marks Range Light..................................14483.5/46458.2

St. Marks River No. 1...................................14480.3/46450.7

Sunken Barge southeast of buoy No. 24..........14441.7/46422.3

Boat Ramps and Marinas

Aucilla River

* The Nutall Rise Landing is located about five miles from the Gulf near the Highway 98 bridge over the Aucilla River. Turn north on the first dirt road east of the bridge. The ramp is a few hundred yards from the highway.

* To reach the lower ramp, turn south off of U.S. Highway 98 one and a half miles east of the bridge over the Aucilla River. Follow the signs. The ramp is about two miles from the Gulf of Mexico. Rocks just out from the base of the ramp can damage a carelessly launched boat, especially at low tide.

Econfina River

The Econfina River boat ramp is at the end of State Highway 14 which crosses Highway 98 about four miles east of the bridge over the Aucilla River. The double ramp is in excellent condition and has docks on both sides. There's a camp store/tackle store and a restaurant nearby.

Econfina on the Gulf has motel rooms and efficiency apartments. R/V and tent camping sites, and a conference center. For information and reservations contact *Econfina On The Gulf*, Rt. 1, Box 255, Lamont, FL 32336; tel. 904-584-5811.

Keaton Beach

To get to Keaton Beach, turn southwest off U.S. Highway 98 onto State Highway 361. The marina is on a canal that exits to a navigation channel leading offshore. Keaton Beach Marina has motel rooms and cottages for rent, a boat hoist and a boat ramp.

Ochlockonee River

*Ochlockonee River State Park: North side of river, entrance to park is about four miles south of Sopchoppy, or about 1 1/2 miles north of the Sopchoppy River Bridge on U.S. Highway 31. Public, paved ramp, and camping sites.

*Cow Creek Landing: South side of river, about one mile east of U.S. Highway 319 on County Road 310. Public, paved ramp.

*Metcalf Landing: On U.S. Highway 98, south side of the river, to the right immediately after crossing the Ochlockonee Bay Bridge, a state park with concrete picnic tables, primitive camping and a sand ramp.

*Bayside Marina: North side of the river, 2 1/2 miles west on County Road 327 off of Highway 98. Privately maintained ramp, boat docks, restrooms, marina and store.

*Ochlockonee Point Landing (Mashes Sand): North side of the river, public landing, paved ramp, 2 1/2 miles east of U.S. Highway 98 on County Road 372. Can be a difficult site to use during low tide.

Spring Creek and Shell Point

Bud's Marina and Fish Camp in Spring Creek: About five miles west of the Wakulla River. From U.S. Highway 98 turn south onto County Road 365, at fork keep to the right; public, concrete ramp.

Shell Point Marina in Shell Point: From U.S. Highway 98 turn south onto County Road 365. At a mile and a half County Road 367 branches off to the left. Follow the signs to the marina; store, restaurant, motel with 20 rooms and six apts., dry storage and slips; paved boat ramp, small launch fee.

St. Marks

The best ramps on the river are in the town of St. Marks which lies at the end of State Road 363 (Woodville Highway) about 16 miles south of Tallahasee.

*Shields Marina has a paved, double ramp with a floating dock. The ramp is privately maintained and there are restrooms, a marina store, and fuel available. There is a small launch fee.

*About a half-mile to the west there's a paved ramp next to Fort San Marcos de Apalache. There is no dock or facilities except a few picnic tables.

*Shell Island Marina, located about a 1/2 mile above the fort on the Wakulla River, has a concrete ramp, bait and tackle store, cabins, a boat hoist and rental boats.

*There is also a ramp in Newport, where U.S. Highway 98 crosses the river. The small, county-maintained concrete ramp is on the east side of the bridge a couple hundred yards down a small dirt lane that turns north off the highway.

St. Marks Refuge

The St. Marks Unit of the St. Marks National Wildlife Refuge is located about 20 miles south of Tallahassee at the end of County Road 59 which intersects U.S. Highway 98, just east of Newport bridge over the St. Marks River. The road runs straight into the entrance gate and on through the refuge to the coast. Just before you reach the lighthouse there is a concrete boat ramp to the right. No facilities are available. There is a small entrance fee at the gate or someone in the group must hold a current Federal Duck Stamp.

Steinhatchee

To get to Steinhatchee from the north, turn west off U.S. Highway 98 onto State Highway 361, a couple miles south of Perry. Turn left at Keaton Beach and continue south. The river appears on your right as you enter the town. From the south, turn west (off of U.S. Highway 98) on State Highway 51, 17 miles north of Shamrock. The roads ends in Steinhatchee. The main public boat ramp is on the Dixie County side of the river in the town of Jena. Plus, all the marinas on the river have either a forklift or a hoist for lowering your boat into the water.

Recipes for Saltwater Fish

McGowan's Plain Ole Fried Fish
(seatrout, cobia, mackerel, etc.)

2 pounds of fish
  (fillets, steaks, or pan dressed)
1 teaspoon salt
dash pepper
1 egg, slightly beaten
salad oil
1 teaspoon milk or water
1 cup bread crumbs,
  cracker crumbs,cornmeal,
  or all purpose flour.

Cut fish into serving size portions. Sprinkle both sides with salt and pepper. Combine egg and milk. Dip fish into egg mixture and roll in crumbs. Place fish in a heated, heavy skillet containing oil. Keep the temperature steady. When fish is brown on one side, turn carefully and brown on the other side. Cooking time should be about 10 minutes, depending on the thickness of the fish. Drain on absorbent paper.
Serves six.

McGowan's Broiled Spanish Mackerel

8 Spanish mackerel fillets
1/2 cup lemon juice
1 tablespoon white wine
2 tablespoons butter
  or margarine
3 drops tabasco sauce
dash of garlic powder
salt and pepper to taste

Lightly oil hinged grill. Salt and pepper fillets. Place fillets on hot grill skin side up. Cook about 3 minutes, carefully turn and baste frequently with heated mixture of lemon juice, wine, tabasco, garlic, and butter. Cook another 5 minutes until done.
Serves four.

McGowan's (Hot) Cocktail Sauce

1/2 cup catchup
2 teaspoons lemon juice
1/2 teaspoon tabasco sauce
1 teaspoon Worcestershire sauce

2 teaspoons mayonnaise
dash black pepper
2 tablespoons prepared horseradish

Combine all the ingredients. Makes about 3/4 of a cup of cocktail sauce.

McGowan's Basil Baked Fish

1/2 pound frozen fish
1 teaspoon Olive oil
1 teaspoon lemon juice
1/4 teaspoon dried basil, crushed
1/8 teaspoon black pepper
2 plum tomatoes, cored and cut crosswise into slices.
2 teaspoon grated, parmesan cheese

Pat fish dry and cut into 2 servings pieces. Combine oil and lemon juice in baking dish. Add fish and coat on both sides. Sprinkle with basil, pepper, and salt. Overlap tomatoes in even layers on fish and sprinkle with parmesan cheese. Cover with foil and bake at 400 degrees for 15 minutes, or until the fish flakes when tested with a fork.

Makes 2 servings.

McGowan's Broiled Shark Steaks

1 1/2 pounds of shark fillets cut 3/4 to 1-inch thick.
3/4 cup mayonnaise
1/2 cup finely chopped cucumber & green onions
1 tablespoon horseradish
salt and pepper

Place shark steaks on a greased piece of foil or a broiler pan. Mix remaining ingredients and spoon over fillets or steaks. Broil about 15 minutes, 4 inches from the heat.

Serves 4.

I recommend marinating shark meat in vinegar, lemon juice, saltwater, or milk to counteract the high concentration of urea in a sharks body. I have tested several recipes without marinating the meat and found no unpleasant ammonia odor, but the meat was always cleaned promptly and without piercing any of the organs. Shark meat should always be immediately placed on ice. B.M.

Tips for Charcoal Grilled Fish

Just about any type of fish can be broiled over a charcoal grill. For best results use a hinged grill to help hold the fish together. The grill should be well greased.

The trick to broiling fish is knowing exactly when to remove it from the heat. The right moment is when the meat turns translucent but is not yet dry. The flesh must separate easily with a fork, but not fall apart. Cook the fish a medium distance from the coals and it will usually be ready-to-eat when the outside turns a light brown. Keeping the meat moist by basting it with herb butter will give it a delicious flavor.

Emergency Numbers

Florida Marine Patrol
(and Resource Protection)..................**488-5757**
Toll free ....**1 + 800-342-5367**

U.S. Coast Guard
(Dial Panama City)...................**1 + 800-342-1821**

Police, Sheriff, Fire, Ambulance/ Paramedics...........................**911**

VHF Radio	Channels
Weather Reports: for receiving NOAA weather reports. No transmission possible.	WX-1, WX-2, WX-3
Calling: for getting the attention of another station or for emergencies.	16
Coast Guard: for talking to the Coast Guard after contacting on 16.	22
Working Channels: Non-commercial for recreational boats only.	9,68,69,71,72,78
Working Channels: Commercial for working boats only	1,7,8,9,10,11,18,19 63,67,79,80,88
U.S. Coast Guard Auxilliary Stations monitor VHF Channel 16 and CB Channel 10. Those stations normally operate from April 1 through October each year.	